CAMBRIDGE

T0344169

AMERICAN EMPOWER

STUDENT'S BOOK B

WITH DIGITAL PACK

A2
ELEMENTARY

Adrian Doff, Craig Thaine
Herbert Puchta, Jeff Stranks, Peter Lewis-Jones

AMERICAN EMPOWER is a six-level general English course for adult and young adult learners, taking students from beginner to advanced level (CEFR A1 to C1). *American Empower* combines course content from Cambridge University Press with validated assessment from the experts at Cambridge Assessment English.

American Empower's unique mix of engaging classroom materials and reliable assessment enables learners to make consistent and measurable progress.

Content you'll love.

Assessment you can trust.

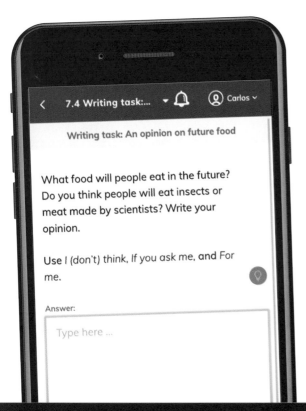

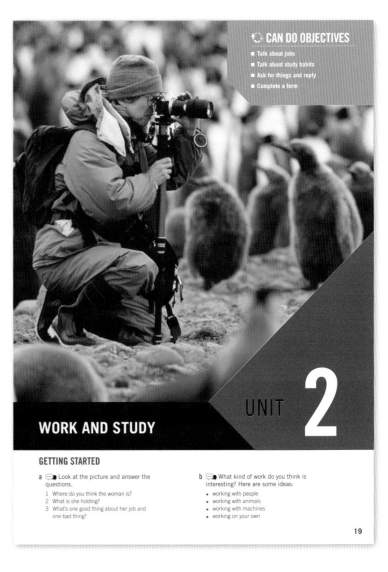

Better Learning with *American Empower*

Better Learning is our simple approach where **insights** we've gained from research have helped shape **content** that drives **results**.

Learner engagement

1 Content that informs and motivates

Insights
Sustained motivation is key to successful language learning and skills development.

Content
Clear learning goals, thought-provoking images, texts, and speaking activities, plus video content to arouse curiosity.

Results
Content that surprises, entertains, and provokes an emotional response, helping teachers to deliver motivating and memorable lessons.

2 Personalized and relevant

Insights
Language learners benefit from frequent opportunities to personalize their responses.

Content
Personalization tasks in every unit make the target language more meaningful to the individual learner.

Results
Personal responses make learning more memorable and inclusive, with all students participating in spontaneous spoken interaction.

> " There are so many adjectives to describe such a wonderful series, but in my opinion it's very reliable, practical, and modern. "
>
> **Zenaide Brianez, Director of Studies, Instituto da Língua Inglesa, Brazil**

Measurable progress

1 Assessment you can trust

Insights
Tests developed and validated by Cambridge Assessment English, the world leaders in language assessment, to ensure they are accurate and meaningful.

Content
End-of-unit tests, mid- and end-of-course competency tests, and personalized CEFR test report forms provide reliable information on progress with language skills.

Results
Teachers can see learners' progress at a glance, and learners can see measurable progress, which leads to greater motivation.

Results of an impact study showing % improvement of Reading levels, based on global *Empower* students' scores over one year.

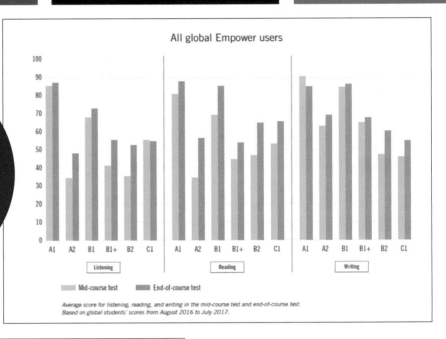

Average score for listening, reading, and writing in the mid-course test and end-of-course test. Based on global students' scores from August 2016 to July 2017.

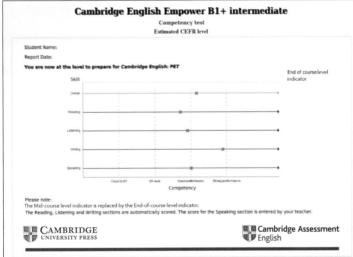

> **We started using the tests provided with Empower and our students started showing better results from this point until now.**

Kristina Ivanova, Director of Foreign Language Training Centre, ITMO University, Saint Petersburg, Russia

2 Evidence of impact

Insights
Schools and colleges need to show that they are evaluating the effectiveness of their language programs.

Content
Empower (British English) impact studies have been carried out in various countries, including Russia, Brazil, Turkey, and the UK, to provide evidence of positive impact and progress.

Results
Colleges and universities have demonstrated a significant improvement in language level between the mid- and end-of-course tests, as well as a high level of teacher satisfaction with *Empower*.

Manageable learning

1 Mobile friendly

Insights
Learners expect online content to be mobile friendly but also flexible and easy to use on any digital device.

Content
American Empower provides easy access to Digital Workbook content that works on any device and includes practice activities with audio.

Results
Digital Workbook content is easy to access anywhere, and produces meaningful and actionable data so teachers can track their students' progress and adapt their lesson accordingly.

> " *I had been studying English for 10 years before university, and I didn't succeed. But now with* Empower *I know my level of English has changed.* "
>
> **Nikita, *Empower* Student, ITMO University, Saint Petersburg, Russia**

2 Corpus-informed

Insights
Corpora can provide valuable information about the language items learners are able to learn successfully at each CEFR level.

Content
Two powerful resources – Cambridge Corpus and English Profile – informed the development of the *Empower* course syllabus and the writing of the materials.

Results
Learners are presented with the target language they are able to incorporate and use at the right point in their learning journey. They are not overwhelmed with unrealistic learning expectations.

Rich in practice

1 Language in use

Insights
It is essential that learners are offered frequent and manageable opportunities to practice the language they have been focusing on.

Content
Throughout the *American Empower* Student's Book, learners are offered a wide variety of practice activities, plenty of controlled practice, and frequent opportunities for communicative spoken practice.

Results
Meaningful practice makes new language more memorable and leads to more efficient progress in language acquisition.

2 Beyond the classroom

There are plenty of opportunities for personalization.

**Elena Pro,
Teacher, EOI
de San Fernando
de Henares,
Spain**

Insights
Progress with language learning often requires work outside of the classroom, and different teaching models require different approaches.

Content
American Empower is available with a print workbook, online practice, documentary-style videos that expose learners to real-world English, plus additional resources with extra ideas and fun activities.

Results
This choice of additional resources helps teachers to find the most effective ways to motivate their students both inside and outside the classroom.

Unit overview

Unit Opener

Getting started page – Clear learning objectives to give an immediate sense of purpose.

Lessons A and B

Grammar and Vocabulary – Input and practice of core grammar and vocabulary, plus a mix of skills.

Digital Workbook (online, mobile): Grammar and Vocabulary

Lesson C

Everyday English – Functional language in common, everyday situations.

Digital Workbook (online, mobile): Listening and Speaking

Unit Progress Test

Lesson D

Integrated Skills – Practice of all four skills, with a special emphasis on writing.

Digital Workbook (online, mobile): Reading and Writing

Review

Extra practice of grammar, vocabulary, and pronunciation. Also a "Review your progress" section for students to reflect on the unit.

Mid- / End-of-course test

Additional practice

Further practice is available for outside of the class with these components.

Digital Workbook (online, mobile)

Workbook (printed)

Components

Resources – Available on cambridgeone.org

- Audio
- Video
- Unit Progress Tests (Print)
- Unit Progress Tests (Online)
- Mid- and end-of-course assessment (Print)
- Mid- and end-of-course assessment (Online)
- Digital Workbook (Online)
- Photocopiable Grammar, Vocabulary, and Pronunciation worksheets

CONTENTS

Contents

WELCOME!

1 FIRST CONVERSATIONS

a ▶ 00.02–00.06 Listen to five short conversations. Match them with pictures a–e.

b ▶ 00.02–00.06 Listen again. Who says these sentences? Match them with pictures a–e.

1. ☐ b ☐ Nice to meet you.
2. ☐ How are you?
3. ☐ What's your name and address?
4. ☐ How do you spell that?
5. ☐ Can we pay, please?
6. ☐ Is that your apartment?

2 SAYING HELLO

a Read Conversation 1. Put the sentences in the correct order.

☐ Hello. Nice to meet you. I'm Pedro.
☐ Hello, Pedro. Nice to meet you.
☐ Hello. I'm Tony, and this is my wife, Joanna.

▶ 00.02 Listen and check your answer.

b 💬 In pairs, say hello and say your name.

c 💬 In groups of four, say hello. Say your name and introduce your partner.

d ▶ 00.03 Read Conversation 2 and complete the sentences. Listen and check your answers.

---
fine   thanks   how

A Hi, Nick. ¹_____ are you?
B I'm ²_____, thanks. And you?
A I'm OK, ³_____.

e 💬 Meet other students. Have a conversation with two or three people in the class.

3 NUMBERS

a ▶ 00.04 Listen to Conversation 3. Complete the bill.

How much do they pay? $ _____

ITEM	NO.	PRICE
COFFEE	(2)	$ ____
ICE CREAM	(2)	$ ____
	Total	$ ____

THANK YOU

b ▶ 00.07 Listen and circle the numbers you hear. Then say all the numbers.

13   15   16   17   12

30   50   60   70   20

c Choose the correct answer.

25 = twenty and five / twenty-five
61 = sixty-one / one and sixty
110 = a hundred ten / a hundred and ten

d Read the numbers aloud. Then say the next three numbers.

1, 2, 3, 4, …   31, 33, 35, …
10, 20, 30, …   50, 100, 150, …
15, 25, 35, …

d Say these colors and spell the words.

e 💬📘 Write two words you know in English. Say the word and ask your partner to spell it.

f ▶00.05 Listen to Conversation 4 and complete the name and address.

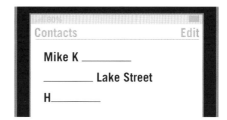

Contacts	Edit
Mike K _____	
_____ **Lake Street**	
H_____	

g 💬📘 Work in pairs. Student A, tell Student B:

• your first and last name   • your address

Student B, ask Student A to spell their name and address. Write the information down. Then switch roles.

How do you spell
your … ?

5 POSSESSIVE ADJECTIVES

a ▶00.06 Read and listen to Conversation 5. Underline the correct answer.

A This is a nice photo. This is *my / your* wife and *his / her* brother.
B Oh, yes. Is that *our / your* apartment?
A Yes, that's *our / their* apartment in San Francisco.
B Mmm, it's very nice.

b Complete the chart.

| our   their   her   his |

I live here.	This is _my_ apartment.
Do you live here?	Is this _your_ apartment?
He lives here.	This is _____ apartment.
She lives here.	This is _____ apartment.
We live here.	This is _____ apartment.
They live here.	This is _____ apartment.

c Complete the sentences with a word from the chart in 5b.

1 This is my brother. _____ name is Jorge.
2 Jenny and Phil are old friends, and that's _____ car.
3 That's a good photo of you. And is that _____ daughter?
4 In this photo, we're on vacation with _____ friends Sue and Bill.
5 I know that girl in the photo. What's _____ name?

4 THE ALPHABET

a ▶00.08 Listen to the letters of the alphabet and say them.

A B C D E F G
H I J K L M N
O P Q R S T U
V W X Y Z

b **Pronunciation** Which letters have … ?

1 the same long sound as s**ee** /i/
2 the same long sound as d**ay** /eɪ/
3 the same short sound as **e**gg /ɛ/

c 💬📘 Test a partner. Student A, point to a letter. Student B, say the letter.

6 CLASSROOM OBJECTS

a Match objects 1–10 with a–j in the picture.

1 a <u>note</u>book	6 a <u>cup</u>board
2 a <u>dic</u>tionary	7 a desk
3 a pro<u>jec</u>tor	8 a <u>white</u>board
4 a <u>ques</u>tion	9 an <u>an</u>swer
5 a pen	10 a <u>text</u>book

b ▶ 00.09 **Pronunciation** Notice the stressed syllable in the words in 6a. Listen, then practice saying the words.

c When do we usually use *an*? Choose the correct answer.
a before *a, e, i, o, u*   b before other letters

d Write *a* or *an* next to each word.

① _____ book	② _____ apple	③ _____ camera
④ _____ glass	⑤ _____ egg	⑥ _____ baby
⑦ _____ box	⑧ _____ ice cream cone	

e Choose one of the words from 6a or 6d. Other students ask questions to guess the word.

Is it big?   No.   Is it white?   No.

f Look at how words change in the plural. Complete the rules.

Singular → Plural	Rule
a pen → pens	Most words add _____ in the plural.
a baby → babies	Change a final *-y* to _____ and add _____.
a glass → glasses	If a word ends in *-s, -x, -sh,* or *-ch,* we add _____.

7 CLASSROOM INSTRUCTIONS

a ▶ 00.10 Listen and follow the instructions you hear. Then listen again. Which verbs do you hear each time?

open   close   look at   read   turn to   write   ask   work

b ▶ 00.11 <u>Underline</u> the correct words. Listen and check.

1 *What's / Who's* this? An apple or an orange?
2 *When's / Where's* Tokyo?
3 *How / What* do you say this word?
4 *Who's / When's* the president?
5 *When's / What's* your English lesson?

c Match questions 1–4 with answers a–d.

1 What's "amigo" in English?   a It's a bag you wear on your back.
2 How do you spell "night"?   b "Duh-bl."
3 What's a "backpack"?   c Friend.
4 How do you say this word?   d N-I-G-H-T.

d Write a question like questions 1–4 in 7c. Then ask other students your question.

CAN DO OBJECTIVES

- Talk about past trips
- Talk about what you like and dislike about transportation
- Say *excuse me* and *I'm sorry*
- Write an email about yourself

UNIT 7

TRIPS

GETTING STARTED

a 💬 Look at the picture and answer the questions.

1 These people are on a trip. What country do you think they're in? Why?
2 Who are the people in the photo: friends or family?
3 What do you think the people talk about?
  - directions
  - the weather
  - personal information
  - shopping
  - their families
  - something else

b 💬 In pairs, ask and answer the questions.

1 Where would you like to travel to?
2 Would you like to travel by … ?
  - car
  - boat
  - plane
  - something else
3 What would you like to see and do there?

7A THE BUS DIDN'T ARRIVE

1 READING

a 💬🗨 Look at the pictures of the three vacation spots. Which countries do you think they are in? Which would you like to go to? Why?

b Read the blog post and match the stories with pictures a–c to find out where they are.

c Read the stories again. Who do you think said each sentence after their trip: Jessica *(J)*, Ethan *(E)*, or Kayla *(K)*?

1 It's not a good idea to buy something cheap.
2 You often see more with your own transportation.
3 It's a good idea to look for transportation information online.
4 It was pretty cold on the water.
5 You sometimes meet interesting people on vacation.
6 If you wear nice clothes, maybe catch a taxi.

d 💬🗨 Which story did you like most? Why?

TRAVEL**BLOG**

Every vacation is a story ... tell us about yours!

Sometimes it's good to miss the bus ...

It was our last day in Cartagena, and my friends and I wanted to go to the beach – Playa Blanca. The receptionist at the hotel gave us a bus schedule. We went to the bus stop, and there was another tourist – Diego, a guy from Brazil. He wanted to go to Playa Blanca, too. We waited and we waited, but the bus didn't arrive. So, Diego checked an app and found out that you can catch a speedboat and get there in 45 minutes. We left the bus stop with Diego and got on a speedboat. It was a really exciting trip and so fast – much better than the bus! We all had so much fun together that day. And, by the way, Diego is now my husband. —Jessica

How to miss the perfect moment ...

I don't really like selfie sticks, but they're useful on vacation. I was in Alaska on vacation with three friends from college. They all had selfie sticks, and I decided to buy one, too. But I didn't want to spend a lot of money, so I got a cheap one. The four of us went on a kayak trip to see Valdez Glacier. There we were: in the water, each person in their kayak – it was a great day. I wanted a memory of this perfect moment, so I put my phone on the selfie stick and ... Well, I didn't buy a very good selfie stick, and my phone fell off. Into the water! I felt so stupid. My friends tried not to laugh, but it was funny, and in the end I laughed, too. —Ethan

Makeup danger ...

Before we went on our vacation to Rome, some friends told us that there's a lot of traffic. They said a good way to get around the city is by scooter. So when my husband and I went to Rome, we didn't use public transportation – we rented two Vespas, the famous Italian scooter. They were great to ride – we got around the city really easily. On the second evening, we decided to go to a nice restaurant for dinner. I put on some nice clothes and makeup – I chose a very red lipstick. But I didn't know about the insects. You see, when you wear lipstick on a scooter, flies and mosquitos stick to your lips. When we got to the restaurant, my lips were covered with them. My husband thought it was very funny. I didn't wear makeup on the scooter again – just very cool sunglasses. –Kayla

2 VOCABULARY Transportation

a Match the words in the box with pictures 1–8.

airplane (plane) scooter speedboat cruise ship
helicopter bus ferry train

b 💬 Which kinds of transportation … ?

- do people often use to go on vacation
- do people normally use to get to work or school
- are unusual for people to use in your country
- do you normally use

c ≫ Now go to Vocabulary Focus 7A on p. 167.

3 GRAMMAR Simple past: negative

a Complete the sentences from Ethan's blog.

1 I _____ want to spend a lot of money.
2 I didn't _____ a very good selfie stick.

b Look at the sentences in 3a and complete the rule.

To make the simple past negative, we use:
_____ + the base form

c Underline more examples of the simple past negative in Jessica's and Kayla's posts.

4 LISTENING

a ▶07.04 Carly and Scott talk about the blog stories and tell another story. Listen and answer the questions.

1 Which blog story did they like?
2 Who tells a story – Carly or Scott?
3 Is the story about transportation or food?

b ▶07.04 Listen again. Underline the correct answers.

1 Carly went to *Mexico City* / *Juarez*.
2 She went with a *friend* / *two friends*.
3 They didn't understand the *waiter* / *menu*.
4 They used *pocket* / *cell phone* dictionaries.
5 The man ordered *food* / *drinks* for the women.
6 The man *left then paid* / *paid then left*.

c 💬 When was a stranger kind to you or someone you know? Tell your partner.

5 GRAMMAR Simple past: questions

a ▶07.05 Complete the questions from Carly and Scott's conversation. Listen and check.

1 _____ you go last year?
2 How _____ you travel there?
3 What _____ you choose?

b Look at the questions in 5a and complete the rule.

To make questions in the simple past, we use:
_____ + subject + base form

c ▶07.05 Pronunciation Listen to the questions in 5a again. Notice the pronunciation of *did you* in each question. Can you hear both words clearly?

d ≫ Now go to Grammar Focus 7A on p. 150.

e ▶07.07 Kayla told a friend about her trip to Italy. Complete the conversation using the verbs in parentheses. Listen and check.

MIKE   How ^{1}_____ (be) your trip to Italy?
KAYLA It ^{2}_____ (be) amazing – incredible!
MIKE   How many cities ^{3}_____ you _____ (visit)?
KAYLA We ^{4}_____ (go) to four: Rome, Florence, Siena, and Venice.
MIKE   How ^{5}_____ you _____ (travel) around Italy?
KAYLA We ^{6}_____ (take) trains, and in Tuscany we ^{7}_____ (rent) a car for three days.
MIKE   What ^{8}_____ you _____ (enjoy) most?
KAYLA The art and the architecture were great, but I ^{9}_____ (love) the food the most. It was delicious!

6 SPEAKING

a Imagine you went on a trip around your country last year. Take notes:

- your opinion of the vacation
- transportation used
- places visited
- what you liked most

b 💬 Work in pairs. Have a conversation like the one in 5e. Ask and answer questions about your vacation.

c 💬 Work in groups. Tell each other about your partner's vacation.

7B | I LIKE THE STATIONS

1 READING

a 💬📱 Which cities do you know that have a subway or express buses?

b Read the article. Match the cities with pictures a–c.

c Read the article again. Which city's transportation system … ?

1 is more than 150 years old
2 is less than 30 years old
3 has good views of the city
4 has interesting stations
5 doesn't use trains
6 do you think is the best

d <u>Underline</u> two things in the article that surprise you. Tell a partner.

e Read "From the locals" and answer the questions.

- Which transportation do you think each post is about?
- Which words tell you the answer?
- Who likes public transportation? Who doesn't?

f 💬📱 In pairs, ask and answer the questions.

- Do you use public transportation? Is it fast?
- What is the best way to get around where you live?

CityTripper.com
Fast City Transportation … Around The World

London The London Underground – the "Tube" – was the first subway system in the world. It opened in 1863. It now has 270 stations, and you can go nearly everywhere in London. It's not cheap, and the trains are often full, but it's unusual because it's very deep under the ground (50 meters in some places). One station, Hampstead, has 320 steps!

Bogotá If you visit Bogotá, there isn't a subway, but you can go on an express bus system called the TransMillenio. It opened in 2000, and there are now 12 lines through the city. The buses travel above ground along main roads. They have a special "line" and platforms, so the city traffic isn't a problem. The buses are very fast, and they're a great way to see the city. They're also very easy to use. You just go across a bridge to the station, pay with a card, and wait for a bus!

Moscow If you visit Moscow, go on the Moscow Metro. It opened in 1935, and the stations are very beautiful, with statues and lamps. Eight million people use it every day, so it can get very crowded. There are police at the stations so it's very safe, even at night. It's also very cheap – you can go across the city for 30 rubles. People on the trains are very polite. They always give their seat to an old person or to anyone with a baby.

From the locals

Sergei *"A good way to get around"*
Most of my friends drive in the city, but I always take the subway. The trains are good, and it's a fast and comfortable way to get around. And I like the stations – they look like palaces!

Antonia *"So easy!"*
I use it to go to work every day, and I love it. The buses come every few minutes, so I don't wait at all. They're clean and they're comfortable, too. And it's a safe way to travel when the roads are busy – I can leave my car at home!

Joanna *"Not much fun"*
I don't really enjoy it. I have to walk up and down over 300 steps because the stations are so deep. In the mornings, the trains are often full, and it's uncomfortable.

2 VOCABULARY
Transportation adjectives

a Find the opposite adjectives in the texts. Write them in the chart.

fast	slow
	dangerous
empty	
comfortable	
	expensive
	dirty

b ▶ 07.08 **Pronunciation** Listen and check your answers. Practice saying the words.

c Which of the adjectives are positive? Which are negative?

d ▶ 07.09 **Pronunciation** Listen to the words and underline the stressed syllable in each word.

comfortable   dangerous   expensive

e 💬🗨 With a partner, take turns being A and B.

  A Make a sentence about transportation with an adjective from 2a.

  B Say you don't agree and use the opposite adjective.

The buses in this town are very expensive.

I don't agree. I think they're pretty cheap.

Bill *"Good, but expensive"*

It's a fast way to get around such a big city, but it's pretty expensive when you use it every day. It's the only fast way to go to work. Sometimes I take a bus and it takes an hour, but on the underground you're there in 15 minutes.

3 GRAMMAR AND LISTENING
Love / like / don't mind / hate + verb + *-ing*

a 💬🗨 When you go to meet a friend, do you usually … ?

  • go by car   • use public transportation   • bike   • walk

b ▶ 07.10 Svetlana and Alex live in Moscow and meet downtown. Listen and complete the chart.

	She came by …	The trip took …
Svetlana		
Alex		

c ▶ 07.10 Listen again. Complete the notes.

	Svetlana thinks	Alex thinks
the Metro is …		
the stations are …		
driving is …		
Alex's / Her car is …		

d ▶ 07.11 Can you remember what Svetlana and Alex said? Complete the sentences with *love*, *like*, *don't mind*, *don't like*, or *hate*. Then listen and check.

1 **SVETLANA**   I _____ going on the Metro.
2 **ALEX**   I _____ using the Metro.
3 **SVETLANA**   I _____ the stations.
4 **ALEX**   I _____ driving in Moscow.
5 **SVETLANA**   I _____ sitting in traffic.
6 **ALEX**   I _____ it, it's not too bad.

e Which verb in 3d means … ?

1 I like it a lot.
2 I don't like it at all.
3 It's OK.

f ≫ Now go to Grammar Focus 7B on p. 150.

4 SPEAKING

a Check (✓) three kinds of transportation that you use.

☐ bus   ☐ train   ☐ subway   ☐ speedboat   ☐ boat   ☐ taxi   ☐ plane

b Take notes about the transportation you checked. Use adjectives from 2a and verbs from 3d.

bus – hate, crowded, slow, dirty

c 💬🗨 Tell your partner about your ideas from 4b. How similar are you?

I hate going on buses. They're always crowded …

7C EVERYDAY ENGLISH
Excuse me, please

Learn to say *excuse me* and *I'm sorry*
- (S) Showing interest
- (P) Emphasizing what we say

1 LISTENING

a  Ask and answer the questions.

1 Do you like going away for the weekend?
2 Where do you like going?
3 What do you like doing there?
4 Do you like going alone or with family and friends?

b Answer the questions about picture a.

1 Where are these people?
2 What are they doing?

c ▶ 07.13 Listen to Part 1 and check your answers in 1b.

d ▶ 07.13 Listen to Issa and Jayden's conversation in Part 1 again and answer the questions.

1 Where is Issa traveling to?
2 What does Issa do to Jayden?
3 How does Jayden react?
  a He is calm.
  b He is angry.
  c He is embarrassed.

e ▶ 07.14 Listen to Part 2. <u>Underline</u> the correct answers.

1 *Issa / Jayden* reserved a window seat.
2 *Issa / Jayden* didn't check the seat numbers.
3 *Issa / Jayden* takes a different seat.

2 USEFUL LANGUAGE
Saying *excuse me* and *I'm sorry*

a Match 1–2 with meanings a–b.

1 Excuse me, please.   a She wants to say there's a problem.
2 Excuse me, but …   b She wants to ask someone to move.

b ▶ 07.15 **Pronunciation** Listen to 1 and 2 in 2a. Notice how the intonation goes down ↘ in 1, but goes down and then up ↘↗ in 2.

c Look at 1 and 2 in 2a. What do you say when … ?

a you want to tell your teacher you don't understand something
b you want to leave the room but another student is in front of the door

d *Very*, *really*, and *so* can all be added to the expression *I'm sorry*. Do you say the words before or after *sorry*?

> I'm sorry I took your seat.

e ▶ 07.16 Match 1–5 with a–e. Listen and check.

1 I'm so sorry I bumped into you.   a I didn't feel well.
2 I'm really sorry I'm late.   b I was in a meeting.
3 I'm sorry I didn't answer your call. c I missed my bus.
4 I'm sorry I didn't come.   d My hands were wet.
5 I'm very sorry I broke your plate.   e I didn't see you.

f Check (✓) the correct replies when people say they're sorry.

1 ☐ That's all right.   4 ☐ Excuse me, please.
2 ☐ That's OK.   5 ☐ Don't worry.
3 ☐ No problem.

g ▶ 07.17 Put sentences a–c and d–f in order to make two short conversations. Listen and check.

a ☐ **A** No problem. They all look the same.
b ☐1☐ **A** Excuse me, but I think that's my coat.
c ☐ **B** Is it? I'm so sorry. I took the wrong one.

d ☐ **A** Don't worry. The seat numbers are hard to read.
e ☐ **B** Oh, I'm sorry. I thought this was number 35.
f ☐1☐ **A** Excuse me, but I think this is my seat.

h In pairs, practice the two conversations in 2g.

3 PRONUNCIATION
Emphasizing what we say

a ▶**07.18** Listen to the sentences in 2e. Notice the stress on the underlined words.

1 I'm <u>so</u> <u>sorry</u> I <u>bumped</u> into you.
2 I'm <u>really</u> sorry I'm <u>late</u>.
3 I'm <u>sorry</u> I didn't <u>answer</u>.
4 I'm <u>sorry</u> I didn't <u>come</u>.
5 I'm <u>very</u> sorry I <u>broke</u> your <u>plate</u>.

b Why are *so*, *very*, and *really* stressed? Choose the best answer.

1 We don't want the other person to hear *sorry* clearly.
2 We want to sound more sorry.
3 We want to speak loudly.

c 💬 Practice saying the sentences in 3a.

4 CONVERSATION SKILLS
Showing interest

a ▶**07.19** Listen to Part 3. Are the sentences true or false?

1 Issa and Jayden are both on their way to Fort Worth.
2 Issa is visiting a friend in Dallas.
3 Jayden went to college in Fort Worth.

b Look at these parts of the conversation from Part 3. Two words aren't correct. Replace them with the words in the box.

Great!	Really?

ISSA Are you visiting Dallas?
JAYDEN No, Fort Worth. I went to college there.
ISSA Right.

ISSA My mom lives there. I go to see her every month.
JAYDEN Oh.

▶**07.19** Listen again and check your answers.

c Why do they say *Great* and *Really*?

1 to say something is true
2 to show they are interested

5 SPEAKING

a 💬 Work in pairs. Use the dialogue map to make a conversation in a coffee shop. Take turns being A and B.

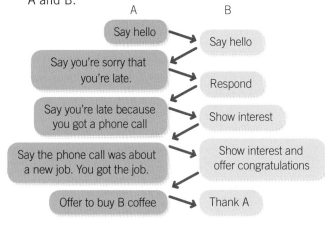

A

- Say hello
- Say you're sorry that you're late.
- Say you're late because you got a phone call
- Say the phone call was about a new job. You got the job.
- Offer to buy B coffee

B

- Say hello
- Respond
- Show interest
- Show interest and offer congratulations
- Thank A

b 💬 In pairs, practice conversations like the one in 5a, but with different reasons for being late. Take turns being A and B.

✅ UNIT PROGRESS TEST

→ **CHECK YOUR PROGRESS**

You can now do the Unit Progress Test.

7D | SKILLS FOR WRITING
It really is hard to choose

1 SPEAKING AND LISTENING

a 💬🔊 You want to stay with a homestay family. What kind of family would you like to stay with? Check (✓) three ideas and tell a partner.

1 ☐ quiet and friendly   5 ☐ lives near a bus/train station
2 ☐ friendly and fun   6 ☐ lives downtown
3 ☐ with young children   7 ☐ has Wi-Fi
4 ☐ with no children   8 ☐ has no TV

b 💬🔊 Read the profiles of two Auckland homestay families. Which family would you like to stay with? Why?

c ▶ 07.20 Alejandro talks to his friend Justin about which family to stay with in Auckland. Does Justin tell Alejandro which family to choose?

d ▶ 07.20 Listen again. Check (✓) the activities that are true for Alejandro.

1 ☐ enjoys gardening
2 ☐ likes watching sports
3 ☐ likes listening to pop music
4 ☐ wants to play rugby
5 ☐ loves going to the beach
6 ☐ wants to study a lot
7 ☐ likes playing soccer
8 ☐ wants to have fun

e 💬🔊 Which family is good for Alejandro? Why?

> I think the Philips family is good because they like sports.

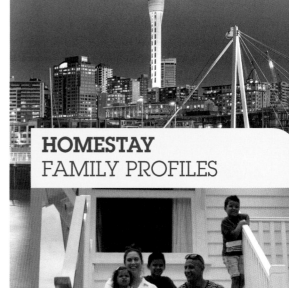

HOMESTAY FAMILY PROFILES

NAME	Joe and Annie Philips
CHILDREN	Jacob (8), Ben (5), and Kate (3)
PETS	no pets
LIKES	swimming, surfing, going to the movies, listening to pop music
LOCATION	near a bus station

NAME	Peter and Sharon Conway
CHILDREN	out of the house
PETS	Sam, our old cat
LIKES	gardening, going for walks, watching all sports
LOCATION	downtown – you can walk to school

2 READING

a Alejandro decided to stay with the Conways. Read his email to them. Check (✓) the main reason he writes to them.

1 ☐ to ask about their house
2 ☐ to tell them about all the sports he likes
3 ☐ to tell them about himself
4 ☐ to explain how much he wants to study

b Read the email again. Number the information in the order you find it.

☐ his future plans ☐ his hobbies
☐ his family's jobs ☐ his hometown

✉ ✎ ☆ ⚑   ⊗

Subject: Homestay

Dear Mr. and Mrs. Conway,

My name is Alejandro Martinez, and I come from Merida, in the Yucatan province of Mexico. Thank you for offering to be my homestay family when I'm in Auckland.

I am 21 years old and study biology in college. I live with my family in Merida. My father is a businessman, and my mother is a doctor. I have one brother and one sister. They're college students, too.

In my free time, I like playing football (I think you say "soccer" in New Zealand!) and meeting my friends. I like watching different kinds of sports with them.

While I'm in Auckland, I really want to study hard and improve my English because I want to become a research biologist after I finish college. I want to study birds. I'd really like to work in a country like New Zealand – I know that you have a lot of very interesting birds there.

I'm looking forward to meeting you when I arrive.

Best wishes,

Alejandro

Merida

3 WRITING SKILLS
Linking ideas with *after*, *when*, and *while*

a <u>Underline</u> the word in each sentence that's different from Alejandro's email.

1 Thank you for offering to be my homestay family while I'm in Auckland.
2 I want to become a research biologist when I finish college.
3 I'm looking forward to meeting you after I arrive.
4 When I'm in Auckland, I really want to study hard.

b Look at the sentences in 3a and complete the rules with the words in the box.

after   beginning   while

1 We use *when* and _____ to connect two activities that happen at the same time.
2 We use *when* and _____ to connect two activities that happen at different times.
3 If the linking word is at the _____ of the sentence, we use a comma (,) between the two parts.

c <u>Underline</u> the correct words. There is more than one possible answer.

1 *After / When / While* I finish my English class, I'd like to go to Canada for a vacation.
2 I'd like to go skiing in the mountains *after / when / while* I'm on vacation.
3 I often play basketball with my colleagues *after / when / while* I finish work.
4 *After / When / While* I watch a game of football, I usually want to play a game myself.
5 My English improved *after / when / while* I was in Sydney.

4 SPEAKING AND WRITING

a Make a list of English-speaking countries you know.

b 💬 Which country in 4a would you like to visit? Why?

I'd like to go to …   I like warm places.   They say the people are friendly.

c Plan an email about yourself to a homestay family in that country. Take notes about:

- your age
- study / job
- what you'd like to do in that country
- free-time interests
- family

d Write your email. Check (✓) each box.

☐ Start the letter with *Dear*
☐ Say thank you
☐ Say who you are
☐ Talk about study / work / free time
☐ Talk about your family
☐ Say what you want to do in the country
☐ Include *I'm looking forward …*
☐ Finish the letter with *Best wishes*
☐ Use *after*, *when*, and *while* to link your ideas

e 💬 Switch emails with another student and check the ideas in 4d.

1 GRAMMAR

a Complete the text with the simple past affirmative or negative form of the verbs in parentheses.

Paul ^{1}_____ (call) a taxi, but it ^{2}_____ (come), so he ^{3}_____ (take) a bus to the airport. The plane ^{4}_____ (be) late, so he ^{5}_____ (wait) for three hours at the airport. The weather ^{6}_____ (be) bad, so the plane ^{7}_____ (land) in a different city. He ^{8}_____ (arrive) at his hotel at 10 p.m. The receptionist ^{9}_____ (ask) him, "Did you have a good trip?" "No, I ^{10}_____ (have) a good trip. It was terrible."

b Write questions about a trip to Mumbai to match the answers.

1 When?   I went there last November.
  When did you go there?
2 How?   I traveled by Air India from London.
3 a good time?   Yes, I had a very nice time.
4 Where?   I stayed in a hotel by the ocean.
5 How long?   I only stayed a week. Then I went to Delhi.
6 hot?   Yes, it was about 35° Celsius.

c 💬 Work in pairs. Choose a place you've visited and ask and answer the questions in 1b. Ask more questions.

d Write sentences about what Clare likes doing. Use the words in the box and a verb + *-ing*.

~~loves~~   likes   doesn't mind   doesn't like   hates
---

1 "Chinese food is fantastic!"
  Clare loves eating Chinese food.
2 "I never listen to Mozart."
3 "I sometimes take the subway. It's OK, but it's not great."
4 "I don't want to watch baseball – it's boring."
5 "I speak French well – it's a nice language."

2 VOCABULARY

a Complete the transportation words.

1 b u s   4 h _ _ i _ _ _ ter
2 tr_ i _   5 f _ _ ry
3 sh _ _   6 sc _ _ ter

b Change the adjectives into their opposites so that the sentences are correct.

1 The bus was almost *full*. There were only three people on it. *empty*
2 I don't like the subway because the stations are so *clean*.
3 I couldn't sleep on the train. It was so *comfortable*.
4 The new train to the airport is very *slow* – only 15 minutes.
5 He's a very *safe* driver. He never looks in the mirror.
6 $100 for a ten-minute trip! That's very *cheap*!

3 WORDPOWER *get*

a Match questions 1–5 with answers a–e.

1 Is Bella still single?   a Thanks. I'll call you when I **get** home.
2 What's the best way to travel downtown?   b Yes, please. Could you **get** some from the fridge?
3 Have a good trip.   c She's fine. I **got** an email from her last night.
4 Do you want milk in your coffee?   d No. She **got** married last year.
5 How's Susie?   e You can **get** the bus.

b Match the word *get* in a–e in 3a with meanings 1–5 below.

1 become   3 travel on   5 take *or* bring
2 receive   4 arrive

c Read the story and answer the questions.

The next morning, Richard ^{a}got another email from the woman named Blanca. It said, ^{b}"Get $3,000 from your bank, put it in a black bag, and then ^{c}get the bus to Morton Street. When you ^{d}get there, walk toward the post office and leave the bag on the steps. Do as I say or things could ^{e}get very bad for you." Richard knew this wasn't a joke – in fact, it was very serious.

1 What do you think happened next?
2 Match the word *get* in the story (a–e) to meanings 1–5 in 3b.

d Match the phrases in the box with a similar phrase in 1–5 below.

---
get a phone call   get a taxi   get an email
get sad   get better   get to the airport
get a glass of water   get the train   get to school
---

1 get angry   4 get to work
2 get a letter   5 get your coat
3 get the bus

e Write four sentences about your life. Use phrases from 3d.

I never get a taxi to the airport.

f 💬 Tell a partner your sentences in 3e. How similar are you?

◯ REVIEW YOUR PROGRESS

How well did you do in this unit? Write 3, 2, or 1 for each objective.
3 = very well   2 = well   1 = not so well

I CAN ...	
Talk about past trips	☐
Talk about what I like and dislike about transportation	☐
Say *excuse me* and *I'm sorry*	☐
Write an email about myself	☐

↻ CAN DO OBJECTIVES

■ Talk about past and present abilities
■ Talk about sports and exercise
■ Talk about the body and getting in shape
■ Talk about health and how you feel
■ Write an article

UNIT **8**

HEALTHY AND IN SHAPE

GETTING STARTED

a 💬🔊 Look at the picture and answer the questions.

1 What country do you think these men are in?
2 What sport do you think this is?
3 Is the game for fun or for a competition?
4 Who do you think took this photo? Why?

b What other sports and exercise would these men like? Make a list.

c 💬🔊 In pairs, share your list. Do you have any of the same sports and exercise?

8A | THEY CAN DO THINGS MOST PEOPLE CAN'T

Learn to talk about past and present abilities
Learn to talk about sports and exercise

G *can / can't, could / couldn't* for ability
V Sports and exercise

1 READING

a 💬 Ask and answer the questions.

1 What famous sporting events do you know?
2 Which athletes do you like? Why?
3 Look at the man in the pictures and answer the questions.
   a What sport does he play?
   b Where's he from?
   c Where is he in the pictures?
   d What would you like to know about him? Write two questions.

b Read the article and check your answers. Does it answer your questions?

c Read the article again. Answer the questions.

1 What was his life like until he was five?
2 How did his life change when he was five?
3 Why were his doctors, friends, and parents surprised?
4 What does the text say about some of the Paralympic athletes?
5 Why is Jonnie famous?

d Underline the parts of the article that surprise you. Tell a partner.

e 💬 Are there any famous Paralympic athletes from your country?

2 GRAMMAR
can / can't, could / couldn't for ability

a Complete the sentences from the article. Check your answers.

1 He _____ run around with the other children anymore.
2 Only 18 months after he lost his leg, he _____ run, swim, and play soccer again.
3 Some of the athletes in the Paralympics _____ walk.
4 But in their sports, they _____ do things that most people _____.
5 _____ you run that fast?

b Complete the rules with the words in the box.

| past   question   present |

To talk about ability, we use *can/can't* for the _____ and *could/couldn't* for the _____.
To make a _____, we change *You can … * to *Can you … ?*

c Look at the question. Which two answers are correct?
Can you run that fast?
a Yes, I do.   b Yes, I can.   c No, I can't.   d No, I don't.

d ▶ 08.01 **Pronunciation** Listen to the sentences in 2a. Can you hear the /l/ sound for the letter *l* in *could* and *couldn't*?

e ≫ Now go to Grammar Focus 8A on p. 152.

Jonnie Peacock
CHAMPION RUNNER

When Jonnie Peacock was five, he was like most boys from his hometown of Cambridge, England – he loved to play sports. Then suddenly his life changed when he became very sick with meningitis. Jonnie's parents took him to the hospital, and he nearly died. The doctors saved his life, but they couldn't save his right leg. He couldn't run around with the other children anymore, and he couldn't play soccer, his favorite sport. In fact, he couldn't play any sports at all. But the doctors gave him a new, artificial leg. He could walk again, but he wanted to do more than that, so he started dancing and playing other sports. His doctors, his friends, and his parents were all surprised that he could do so much. Only 18 months after he lost his leg, he could run, swim, and play soccer again, but running was his best sport. In 2010, Jonnie started to practice a lot. He wanted to go to the London 2012 Paralympics, the Olympic Games for disabled athletes. Some of the athletes in the Paralympics can't walk, and some can't see at all or can't see very well. But in their sports, they can do things that most people can't. Jonnie Peacock won a gold medal at the London 2012 Paralympic Games when he was only 19 years old. He ran the 100 meters in a time of 10.90 seconds! He won another gold medal at the 2016 Paralympic Games in Rio de Janeiro, Brazil, with an even faster time of 10.81 seconds! He still enjoys dancing, as well. In 2017, Jonnie was the first amputee paralympian to compete on the TV show *Strictly Come Dancing*.

CAN YOU RUN THAT FAST?

3 LISTENING

a 💬🔊 Talk to other students. Try to find a student who … .

1 often goes running
2 never goes running
3 once ran in a marathon or a half-marathon
4 exercises once a week or more

b Read the information about the podcast. What is your answer to the question in the title?

FOCUS ON SPORTS

IS RUNNING GOOD FOR YOU?

This weekend, 25,000 people are running in the Los Angeles marathon. But is running good for you? And how far is it safe to run? We talk to sports trainer Hanna Freeman.

🔊 LISTEN

c ▶️ 08.03 Listen to the podcast. What does Hanna think … ?

1 is good for you
2 is not good for you

d ▶️ 08.03 Listen again. Complete the notes below.

Rule No. 1: Don't _____.
            At the start, run _____.
Rule No. 2: _____ a lot of _____.
            When you run, you _____.
Rule No. 3: Listen _____.
            If you feel tired, _____.
            If your foot hurts, _____.
Rule No. 4: _____!

e 💬🔊 In groups, talk about other ways you know to stay in shape. How many can you list?

4 VOCABULARY Sports and exercise

a Match the words in the box with the pictures a–f.

do yoga   play badminton   ride a bike   dance   skate   ski

b ⯈⯈ Now go to Vocabulary Focus 8A on p. 167 for sports and exercise collocations.

c Read the sentences. Put them in order from good (1) to bad (4).

a ☐ I can play baseball pretty well.
b ☐ I can't play baseball very well.
c ☐ I can play baseball really well.
d ☐ I can't play baseball at all.

d 💬🔊 Ask and answer questions about the activities in 4a.

> Can you ski?
>
> Yes, I can ski very well.
>
> I can't ski at all.

5 SPEAKING

a Think about sports or other free-time activities. Write sentences about … .

• one thing you can do well
  I can …
• one thing you can't do at all, but you'd like to learn
  I can't …
• one thing you could do well when you were a child
  I could …
• one thing you couldn't do very well as a child
  I couldn't …

b 💬🔊 Ask other students if they can or could do the same things.

> Can you dance the samba?
>
> Could you swim well when you were a child?
>
> No, I can't! Can you?
>
> Very well, yes.

c 💬🔊 Who can or could do the same things? Who would like to do the same things?

> Sachiko and I can play tennis pretty well.
>
> Mia and I would like to learn to snowboard.

8B | HOW EASY IS IT TO GET IN SHAPE?

Learn to talk about the body and getting in shape

G *have to / don't have to*

V Parts of the body; Appearance

1 READING

a 💬🔊 Ask and answer the questions.
1 What do you think are good ways of getting in shape?
2 What exercise do you do?
3 Would you like to do more or less exercise? Why?

b Read the first paragraph of the article. Answer the questions in the article.

c 💬🔊 What do you think the new type of exercise is? Read the rest of the article to find out. Were you correct?

d Complete the HIIT fact sheet.

e 💬🔊 Talk about the questions.
1 Would you like to try HIIT? Why / Why not?
2 Do you think it works? Why / Why not?

2 GRAMMAR *have to / don't have to*

a Complete the sentences from the text with the words in the box. Use some words more than once.

have	don't	to

1 You _____ _____ run as fast as you can.
2 You _____ _____ _____ spend hours and hours in the gym.
3 What do you _____ _____ do?

b Sentences a–c talk about the sentences in 2a. Underline the correct answers.
a In sentence 1, you *need to / don't need to* run as fast as you can.
b In sentence 2, you *need to / don't need to* spend hours in the gym.
c Sentence 3, asks what you *need to / don't need to* do.

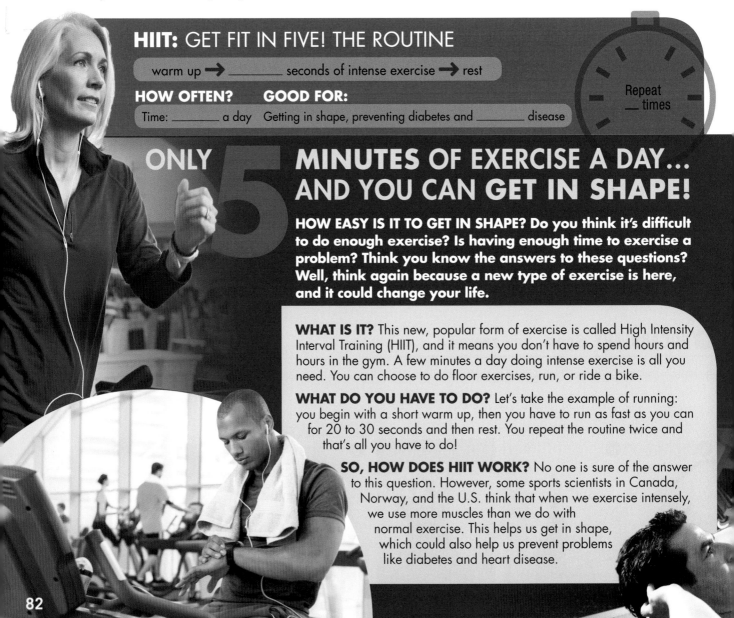

HIIT: GET FIT IN FIVE! THE ROUTINE

warm up → _____ seconds of intense exercise → rest

HOW OFTEN?   **GOOD FOR:**

Time: _____ a day   Getting in shape, preventing diabetes and _____ disease

Repeat __ times

ONLY 5 MINUTES OF EXERCISE A DAY... AND YOU CAN GET IN SHAPE!

HOW EASY IS IT TO GET IN SHAPE? Do you think it's difficult to do enough exercise? Is having enough time to exercise a problem? Think you know the answers to these questions? Well, think again because a new type of exercise is here, and it could change your life.

WHAT IS IT? This new, popular form of exercise is called High Intensity Interval Training (HIIT), and it means you don't have to spend hours and hours in the gym. A few minutes a day doing intense exercise is all you need. You can choose to do floor exercises, run, or ride a bike.

WHAT DO YOU HAVE TO DO? Let's take the example of running: you begin with a short warm up, then you have to run as fast as you can for 20 to 30 seconds and then rest. You repeat the routine twice and that's all you have to do!

SO, HOW DOES HIIT WORK? No one is sure of the answer to this question. However, some sports scientists in Canada, Norway, and the U.S. think that when we exercise intensely, we use more muscles than we do with normal exercise. This helps us get in shape, which could also help us prevent problems like diabetes and heart disease.

c ▶ 08.06 **Pronunciation** Listen to sentences 1 and 2 in 2a and answer the questions.

1 How does the speaker say *v* in *have*: /v/ or /f/?
2 How does the speaker say *to* – is it stressed or unstressed?

d ≫ Now go to Grammar Focus 8B on p. 152.

e Work on your own. Think about things you have to do in your life. Write four sentences. Think about:

- daily routine
- work
- study
- family
- pets

I have to take our family dog for a walk every morning.

f 💬 Tell a partner about things you have to do. Ask more questions.

> I have to clean my house every weekend.

> Do you have to clean all the rooms?

3 LISTENING

a 💬 Look at pictures a and b and answer the questions with a partner.

1 What kind of exercise is this?
2 Do you think it's easy or difficult?

b ▶ 08.08 Listen to Stella and then Mariana talk about exercise. Match the speakers with pictures a and b.

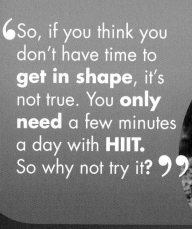

6So, if you think you don't have time to **get in shape**, it's not true. You **only need** a few minutes a day with **HIIT.** So why not try it?**99**

c ▶ 08.08 Listen again. Are the sentences true or false? Correct the false sentences.

1 Stella thinks yoga is good for everyone.
2 Her favorite yoga exercise is easy to do.
3 She practiced doing this exercise for a long time.
4 Mariana thinks beginner yoga is easy.
5 She has to think carefully when she does yoga.
6 She doesn't like the end of each yoga lesson.

4 VOCABULARY Parts of the body

a Match the words in the box with the parts of the body in the picture.

leg back foot head neck
stomach arm hand finger toe

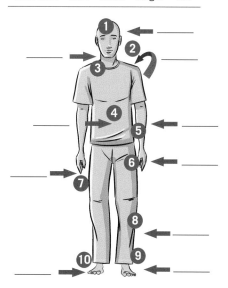

b 💬 Talk about the questions.

1 Which parts of the body can you break?
2 Which parts of the body often give people problems?

c ≫ Now go to Vocabulary Focus 8B on p. 168 for appearance vocabulary.

5 SPEAKING

a Look at activities 1–5 and choose one. Think of things people have to do and have to have if they want to do this activity. Take notes.

1 run a marathon
   go running every day   *have strong legs*
2 climb a mountain
3 swim a long way
4 dance for 24 hours
5 ride a bike along the Pacific Coast Highway

b 💬 Tell your partner what people have to do to get ready for your activity and what they have to have. Don't tell them what your activity is. Can your partner guess?

> You have to go running every day, and you have to have strong legs.

8C EVERYDAY ENGLISH
I'm a little tired

1 LISTENING

a 💬🗨 Answer the questions about the pictures.

1 Where are Alex and Kate?
2 How do you think Alex feels?
3 Do you think Kate is in good shape?
4 Imagine what Kate might say to Alex.

b ▶**08.11** Listen to Part 1 and check your answers. What does Kate tell Alex to do?

c ▶**08.12** Listen to Part 2 and answer the questions.

1 What's Alex's problem?
   a He has a headache.
   b His back hurts.
   c He needs to eat some food.
   d He has a fever.
2 What do you think Alex wants to do?
   a go to the dance class with Kate
   b go home
   c run on the treadmill again

2 USEFUL LANGUAGE
Talking about health and how you feel

a Complete the mini-conversations. Use the words and phrases in the box.

the matter   feel well   look so good   'm a little tired   all right

KATE Are you ¹_____?
ALEX I think so.

KATE You don't ²_____.
ALEX Yes, I ³_____.

KATE What's ⁴_____?
ALEX I'm not sure. I don't ⁵_____.

b ▶**08.11–08.12** Listen to Parts 1 and 2 again and check your answers in 2a.

c Look at some ways to say how you feel.

I'm **tired**.   I have **a headache**.   My **back** hurts.

Which of the words in the box can you use instead of the words in **bold**?

a stomachache   a cold   sick   hungry
arm   foot   a toothache   a fever

d 💬🗨 In pairs, take turns asking about health and saying how you feel. Use the phrases from 2a and 2c.

3 CONVERSATION SKILLS
Expressing sympathy

a Complete what Kate says with the words in the box.

bad	sorry	no

ALEX Actually, I feel awful.
KATE Oh [1]_____. Come and sit down.

ALEX I don't feel well.
KATE I'm [2]_____ to hear that.

KATE You had nothing to eat all day?
ALEX I … well … um … no. It was a busy day.
KATE That's too [3]_____. Well, I'm not surprised you don't feel well.

b What do Kate's phrases in 3a mean?
  1 I feel sorry for you.
  2 I don't feel sorry for you.

c In pairs, take turns saying these sentences and giving sympathy using phrases from 3a.
  1 I have a cold.
  2 I'm so tired.
  3 My back hurts.
  4 I feel really sick.
  5 I lost all my money.
  6 My best friend is mad at me.

4 PRONUNCIATION Connecting words

a ▶ 08.13 Listen to the sound of the letters in **bold** in these sentences. Then read the sentence below and underline the correct words.

  1 Come and si**t** down.
  2 Jus**t** take a break.
  3 Don'**t** tell me …
  4 Goo**d** to see you.

The sound *connects* / *doesn't connect* with the next word, and there's *a* / *no* pause.

b In pairs, take turns saying the sentences in 4a and giving a reply.

> Come and sit down.

> OK, thank you.

1 Student B doesn't look good. Ask him/her what's the matter. When he/she tells you, show sympathy using expressions like *Oh no!* or *That's too bad!*
Then ask if he/she has a fever. Tell him/her what to do, e.g., *See a doctor. Go to bed.*

b **Conversation 2.** Now look at your second card. Think about what you want to say. Then listen to Student B and reply.

2 You're not feeling very well. You have a stomachache and your eyes hurt. You don't feel hungry. When Student B asks you, tell him/her what's the matter.

5 SPEAKING

a ≫ **Communication 8C** Student A look at the information below. Student B go to p. 134.

Conversation 1. Read your first card. Think about what you want to say. Then start the conversation with Student B.

✓ UNIT PROGRESS TEST

→ **CHECK YOUR PROGRESS**

You can now do the Unit Progress Test.

8D SKILLS FOR WRITING
However, I improved quickly

1 SPEAKING AND LISTENING

a 💬🔊 Ask and answer the questions.

1 Which of these free-time activities are popular in your country? Which aren't popular in your country? Why not?
   - playing chess
   - going dancing
   - riding a bike
   - playing video games
   - looking for interesting insects
   - hiking

2 What other activities are popular in your country?

b Read the email Andy and Gina get at work and answer the questions.

1 What's the problem with the company blog?
   a There's too much information.
   b It's kind of boring.
2 What kind of information can the staff put in their articles?
   a information about their free time
   b information about their day at work

c ▶ 08.14 Andy talks to Gina about his free-time activity. Listen and answer the questions.

1 Which activity in 1a does Andy talk about?
2 Does he want to write an article about it?

d ▶ 08.14 Listen again. Match 1–6 with a–f.

1 A year ago, …
2 Two weeks after his first bike ride, …
3 A couple of months ago, …
4 Last weekend, …
5 Almost every day, …
6 You always …

a he bought a bike.
b a car hit him.
c he rides his bike.
d he rode in the hills for two days.
e have to be careful in traffic.
f a friend invited him for a bike ride.

Our staff blog

From: The management team
To: All staff

We want to try to make the company blog more interesting. We would like to find out more about you, the people who work for this company. We'd love to hear about what you do in your free time. Write a short article and send it to us with a photo so we can put it on the blog.

e Think of something you do in your free time. Take notes. Use the questions to help you.

1 When did you start doing this activity?
2 What's something important you did when you started?
3 What do you normally do?
4 What is something interesting you did recently?

f 💬🔊 Ask and answer questions about your activities.

I bought a chess set two months ago.

Was it expensive?

I found a very unusual stamp last month.

Where is the stamp from?

2 READING

a Read Dylan's article for the company blog. Check (✓) what's the same about Dylan's and Andy's activities.

1 ☐ they do their free-time activities outdoors
2 ☐ they do their free-time activities every day
3 ☐ they get in shape doing their free-time activities
4 ☐ they hurt their feet recently

b Read the article again. Are the sentences true or false? Correct the false sentences.

1 Three years ago, Dylan was lonely.
2 He liked the idea of hiking immediately.
3 Hiking was a little difficult at first.
4 He met his wife on a hike.
5 It's very difficult to learn how to go hiking.

OUR STAFF:
working hard, playing hard

Walking my way to love by Dylan Jones

Three years ago, I started working for this company. I didn't know anyone in the area, so I decided to do some exercise to meet new people. However, I was really out of shape. I tried doing different kinds of sports, but I did them all badly. I found an answer to all my problems by going for a walk.

A colleague of mine invited me to go on a hike in the mountains. I didn't say yes immediately because it didn't sound very interesting. However, I decided it could be good exercise for me, so I went along. This was the beginning of my love of hiking.

At first, I had to walk slowly because I wasn't in very good shape. However, I improved quickly, and now I can walk pretty fast for hours. I began to feel so much better. While I was on a hike with a group of people one weekend, I met Marina. She's now my wife. We go hiking once or twice a month, and we love it.

You don't have to do anything special to start hiking. You only have to know how to walk, and most people can do that. However, you have to buy special boots so you don't hurt your feet. Hiking is a great way to enjoy our beautiful country. And you never know – perhaps you can find true love, too!

Me on a hike!

3 WRITING SKILLS
Linking ideas with *however*; adverbs of manner

a Notice the underlined word that links the ideas in two sentences together.

I didn't say yes immediately because it didn't sound very interesting. <u>However</u>, I decided it could be good exercise for me, so I went along.

Is the idea in the second sentence surprising after reading the idea in the first sentence?

b <u>Underline</u> three more sentences in Dylan's article linked by *however*. What punctuation do we use after this word?

c Match the sentences. Link each pair with *however*.

1 I can only do very simple exercises.
2 I started doing yoga about six years ago.
3 I fell off my bike and hurt my leg.

a I didn't stop riding.
b I can't do the difficult positions.
c I feel really in shape.

d Notice the underlined adverb of manner in the sentence. Does it tell us what Dylan did or how he did it?

I tried doing different kinds of sports, but I did them all <u>badly</u>.

e Circle the adverbs in Dylan's article that go with these verbs.

1 walk (x2)   2 improve

f We make most adverbs of manner by adding *-ly* to an adjective.

clear   + -ly   = clearly

Which adverb in Dylan's article is different?

4 WRITING

a Plan an article about your free-time activity. Use your ideas in 1e. Think of:

• an interesting way to begin your article
• something you have to or don't have to do with your hobby

b Write your article. Use adverbs of manner.

c Switch articles with another student and check that:

☐ the beginning is interesting
☐ there's useful information about the hobby
☐ the article uses adverbs of manner

1 VOCABULARY

a Complete the sentences with the words in the box.

> yoga   dance   bike   badminton   baseball   ski

1 When I went to the U.S., I learned to play _____.
  I wasn't very good at it because I could never hit the ball.
2 On my last winter vacation, I went to the mountains and
  learned how to _____. It was a lot of fun.
3 On the weekends, my favorite form of exercise is to get on
  my _____ and go for a ride in the country.
4 I often meet my friend for a game of _____.
  We always play indoors.
5 I'd like to join a _____ class and learn the waltz and
  the tango. It's a fun way to stay in shape and make friends.
6 The strange thing about _____ is that you have to
  stay in the same position for a long time.

b Complete the words for parts of the body.

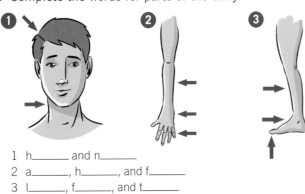

1 h_____ and n_____
2 a_____, h_____, and f_____
3 l_____, f_____, and t_____

2 GRAMMAR

a Complete the text with *can*, *can't*, *could*, or *couldn't*.

In my family, we love playing sports. I ¹_____ play badminton
well, and my sister ²_____ ski well. When we were children,
we ³_____ both play soccer very well, but we're both too
slow now. The only sport I ⁴_____ do is swimming. I didn't
learn to swim. My sister did, and she ⁵_____ swim very
fast – 50 meters in about 40 seconds. We also tried to learn
musical instruments. I studied the guitar, but I ⁶_____ play
well at all. I was always too busy playing sports.

b Complete the sentences with the correct form of
have to.

1 If you want to go running, you _____ buy
  comfortable running shoes.
2 You _____ go to the gym every day – three
  times a week is enough.
3 _____ I _____ use the same
  machines every time I go to the gym?
4 You _____ take a small towel with you when
  you go to the gym.
5 He _____ be careful on his bike. Last year he
  had a bad accident.

3 WORDPOWER *tell / say*

a Match sentences 1–3 with pictures a–c.
  1 My grandmother **told** us **stories** when we were children.
  2 What did you **say** to me? I didn't hear you.
  3 **Say hello** to your parents when you get there.

b Notice the words in **bold** in the sentences in 3a.
Complete the phrases with *say* or *tell*.
  1 _____ hello / goodbye / thank you / I'm sorry
  2 _____ a story / the truth / a joke

c Complete the sentences with *to* if it's possible.
  1 She told _____ me she doesn't feel well.
  2 They said _____ me that they come from Argentina.
  3 I'm sure he told _____ the truth.
  4 We said thank you _____ them when we left.
  5 Can you tell _____ me what time it is?

d Complete the sentences with the words in the box.

> truth   you   sorry   thanks   me   story

  1 Could you please tell the children a bedtime _____?
  2 My wife told _____ she likes living here.
  3 I don't think that's right. He didn't tell us the _____.
  4 I just want to say _____ for a great dinner last night.
  5 Please say you're _____ to Julia for not going to
    her party.
  6 Yesterday I told _____ to arrive on time, but you're half
    an hour late.

e Complete the sentences with your own ideas.
  1 When I was a child, _____ told me stories about ...
  2 The last person I said sorry to was _____ because ...
  3 I always say thank you to ...
  4 ... tells really funny/bad jokes.

f 💬 Tell a partner your ideas from 3e.

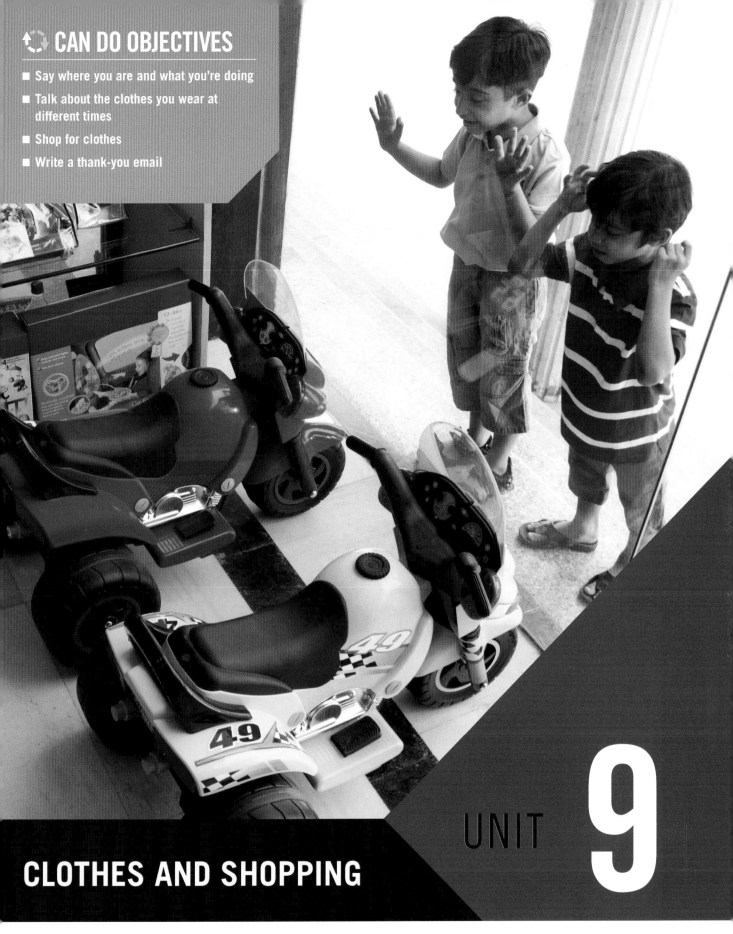

UNIT 9

CLOTHES AND SHOPPING

GETTING STARTED

a 💬🗨 Look at the picture and answer the questions.

1 What are the boys doing?
2 What do these boys talk about? What questions do they ask?
3 Do you think these boys enjoy shopping?

b 💬🗨 Where's the best place to go shopping in your town or city for … ?

- food
- clothes
- a present for someone

9A | WE'RE NOT BUYING ANYTHING

Learn to say where you are and what you're doing

G Present continuous

V Shopping; Money and prices

1 VOCABULARY Shopping

a Match pictures 1–6 with the words in the box.

> a drugstore   a department store   a fast food restaurant
> a bookstore   a clothing store   a coffee shop

💬 Which of these stores is your favorite? Why?

b Look at the map of the shopping mall. Match the words with a–f in the map.

> stairs   entrance   parking lot   bus stop
> information desk   ATM

c ▶09.01 **Pronunciation** Listen to the words. Which word is stressed: the first word or the second word?

- clothing store
- department store
- parking lot
- information desk
- bus stop

d Where can these people go in the shopping mall?

1 "My son needs new jeans."
2 "Let's get a new couch."
3 "I want something to read on the plane."
4 "I have a headache. I need some aspirin."
5 "Can you take my bags to the car?"
6 "Are you hungry? I need to eat!"
7 "I don't have any money."

e ≫ Now go to Vocabulary Focus 9A on p. 169. for money and prices vocabulary.

2 LISTENING

a 💬🔊 When you meet friends in town, what do you usually do? Here are some ideas:

- go shopping
- go to a coffee shop
- go to the movies
- go for a walk

b A group of friends want to go to the movies together. Look at the shopping mall. Where is a good place to meet?

c ▶09.03 Listen to Conversation 1. Where does Sam want to meet Addie? What do you think will happen?

d ▶09.04 Listen to the next two phone conversations. Underline the correct answers.

Conversation 2
1 Sam is *in the bookstore* / *in the coffee shop*.
2 Addie is *at the bus stop* / *in the parking lot*.

Conversation 3
3 Amy is *in the clothing store* / *in the department store*.
4 Diego is *at the information desk* / *at the ATM*.

e 💬🔊 Look at the pictures and answer the questions with a partner.

1 Why do you think Sam is looking at his watch?
2 How do you think Addie feels? Why?

f ▶09.05 Listen to Conversation 4 and check your answers.

Sam

Addie

3 GRAMMAR Present continuous

a ▶09.06 Match the questions and the answers from the conversations. Listen and check your answers.

1 Where are you?
2 Are you getting a coffee?
3 Where are you waiting for us?
4 Are you buying furniture?

a I'm standing by the entrance.
b I'm just getting some cash.
c No, we're not buying anything.
d No, I'm just buying that new book.

b Choose the correct words to complete the rule.

We use *be* + verb + *-ing* to talk about … .   a now   b all the time

c Complete the charts with the correct form of the verbs in the box.

talk   wait   read   park   drink

Affirmative (+)		Negative (−)	
I'm We're He's / She's	___ a magazine. ___ on the phone.	I'm not We're not / We aren't He's not / He isn't She's not / She isn't	___ coffee. ___ at the entrance.

Yes/No questions (?)	
Are you Is he / she	___ the car?

d ▶09.07 **Pronunciation** Listen to the sentences and notice the stress.

1 I'm standing by the entrance.
2 We're waiting for you.
3 We're not buying anything.
4 Are you getting a coffee?
5 Where are you waiting for us?

Listen again and repeat.

e ≫ Now go to Grammar Focus 9A on p. 154.

f Work on your own.

1 Think of three places in your town or city, but don't tell your partner.
2 Write a sentence to say what you are doing in each place.

g 💬🔊 Listen to your partner's sentences. Guess where he/she is.

I'm eating a burger.

Are you in a fast food restaurant?

4 SPEAKING

a ≫ **Communication 9A** Student A go to p. 134. Student B go to p. 136.

9B | EVERYONE'S DANCING IN THE STREETS

Learn to talk about the clothes you wear at different times

G Simple present or present continuous
V Clothes

1 READING

a 💬🔊 Talk about when you shop for food, clothes, and other things.

- before work/class
- at lunchtime
- at night
- on the weekends

b José is from Mexico and Diana is from Texas, in the U.S. Read the social media posts and answer the questions. Write José (*J*), Diana (*D*), or both (*B*).

Who writes about … ?

a studying   c work
b small stores   d shopping malls

c Read the posts again. Are the sentences true or false? Correct the false sentences.

1 José only speaks Mandarin at work.
2 The Chinese people he knows like shopping.
3 José would like to go to a party.
4 Diana doesn't like Venice in the winter.
5 She likes the stores in Venice.
6 It's very quiet in Venice this week.

d Read the messages below. Which one is José's and which one is Diana's?

e 💬🔊 Talk about the questions.

1 Which festival would you like to go to? Why?
2 Do you have festivals like these in your country? What do people do?

Friends Abroad

JOSÉ Message posted: 18:36   Send José a message 💬

Hi everyone! I'm really enjoying life here in Shanghai. My new job is pretty busy, but my coworkers are very friendly, and they all speak English to me. In my free time, I sometimes study Mandarin and relax. I often go shopping because this is a popular "hobby" here. I usually meet friends at a mall. Right now, it's Chinese New Year here. My friends told me there's a great street party this evening – I really want to go.

DIANA Message posted: 12:23   Send Diana a message 💬

Hello to all my friends. I love it here in Venice! It's so beautiful – even in the winter. I have to spend a lot of time on my art history classes, but on the weekends I get some free time. I usually walk around and look at the old buildings, or when it's cold, I go to museums. There are so many interesting little stores here, too – it's great. It's very different from going to a mall. This week it's Carnevale, and the whole city is like one big party. Yesterday my friends invited me to a big party in a *piazza* (that's Italian for a town square). It's tonight, and I have to wear a long dress and mask. I need to go shopping!

We're all out in the street. We're watching a big, beautiful dragon go by. And everyone's wearing red – even me!

Everyone's dancing in the streets and having a great time. We're all wearing amazing clothes – I'm even wearing a dress!

2 GRAMMAR
Simple present or present continuous

a Read the sentences from José's online post and message. Match them with meaning a or b.

1 I usually meet friends at a mall.
2 We're watching a big, beautiful dragon.

a José's normal routine   b Happening to José now

b Complete the rule with the correct tense.

present continuous	simple present

We use the _____ to talk about things we usually do.
We use the _____ to talk about things that happen right now.

c Underline more examples of the simple present and present continuous in Diana's online post and message.

d ≫ Now go to Grammar Focus 9B on p. 154.

e ▶09.09 Complete the conversation with the correct form of the verbs in parentheses. Listen and check.

JOSÉ Hello?
JUAN Hi, José! Are you busy?
JOSÉ Hi! Yes, I ¹_____ (get) ready to go out to a street party.
JUAN Oh, sorry. I can call back.
JOSÉ OK, thanks. I usually ²_____ (not go) out much during the week, but it's New Year.
JUAN Of course.
JOSÉ Sorry, Juan. My friends ³_____ (arrive). I have to go now. We can talk later.

3 LISTENING & VOCABULARY Clothes

a ▶09.10 Tina read José's post and called him. Pete read Diana's post and called her. Listen to the conversations. Why are Tina and Pete surprised?

1 Tina thinks that José doesn't like … .
   a parties
   b wearing red
   c going out at night
2 Pete thinks that Diana doesn't like … .
   a going out for dinner
   b being in photos
   c wearing dresses

b ▶09.10 Listen again and check (✓) the clothes words you hear.

socks · shoes · boots · scarf · pants · shirt · dress · earrings · jeans · gloves · raincoat · sweater

c Pronunciation The words in the chart all have the letter *o* but have a different sound. Write *shoe* in the correct column.

Sound 1 /ɑ/	Sound 2 /u/	Sound 3 /ʌ/	Sound 4 /oʊ/
sock	boot	glove	coat

d ▶09.11 Write these words in the chart in 3c. Listen and check your answers.

come   shop   know   mother   group   box   phone   two

e ≫ Now go to Vocabulary Focus 9B on p. 168.

4 SPEAKING

a Think of someone in your family or a friend that you saw earlier today. What's this person wearing today? What color are their clothes? Take notes.

b 💬 Tell your partner what this person is wearing.

> Today my friend Louise is wearing dark blue jeans with brown boots.

> My brother's at work today. He's wearing black pants and an orange shirt. He's also wearing black shoes.

9C EVERYDAY ENGLISH
It looks really good on you

Learn to shop for clothes
- **S** Saying something nice
- **P** Connecting words

1 LISTENING

a 💬 Ask and answer the questions.

1 How often do you buy clothes?
2 Which sentence a–c describes you best?
   a I love buying clothes. I buy something new every week.
   b I only buy clothes if I really need them.
   c I don't buy clothes often, but I like looking around clothing stores.

b ▶ 09.15 Listen to Part 1. Who wants to buy clothes: James, Daniela, or both?

c ▶ 09.15 Change three incorrect things in the text below. Listen to Part 1 again to check your answers.

> James is meeting Camila to go to a concert. He wants to wear new clothes as a surprise. Daniela says she's free at 12:00. She isn't happy about it.

d ▶ 09.16 Listen to Part 2 and answer the questions.

1 What clothes does James want to buy?
2 What size does James wear?
3 Do you think James enjoys shopping?

e 💬 Do you ever ask friends or family to help you buy clothes? Who do you ask and why?

2 USEFUL LANGUAGE Choosing clothes

a Match 1–4 with a–d.

1 What are you looking for?
2 What size are you?
3 What color would you like?
4 Why don't you try them on?

a In pants? 34 in the waist.
b Oh, I don't know. Something dark?
c A shirt and pants.
d OK. Excuse me, where are the fitting rooms?

b ▶ 09.16 Listen to Part 2 again and check your answers in 2a.

c 💬 In pairs, practice saying the questions and answers in 2a.

d 💬 Take turns helping your partner choose clothes.

A You want a jacket.   B You want a pair of jeans.

3 LISTENING

a ▶ 09.17 Listen to Part 3 and answer the questions.

1 Does Daniela like the clothes James tries on?
2 What does James think about the pink shirt?

b ▶ 09.17 Listen Part 3 again and complete James's receipt.

NORMAN'S FOR CLOTHES

ITEM	NO.	PRICE
SHIRT	1	$49.99
PANTS	1	$ _____
	Total	$ _____

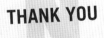

THANK YOU

4 USEFUL LANGUAGE
Paying for clothes

a ▶09.18 Listen and correct a mistake in each sentence.

1 I take them.
2 How much these are?
3 Should I put the receipt on the bag?

b Read this conversation in a clothing store. Add one word in each blank.

A Can I ¹_____ you?
B Yes, how ²_____ are these sunglasses?
A They're $29.99.
B OK, I'll ³_____ them. Can I pay by credit ⁴_____?
A No, sorry, only cash. But there's an ATM right over there.
B OK, thanks. I'll be right back.

c 💬 In pairs, practice the conversation in 4b, but with different clothes. Take turns being A and B.

5 CONVERSATION SKILLS
Saying something nice

a Read what Daniela says. Add the same verb to both sentences.

1 That _____ great.
2 It _____ really good on you.

b Which sentence could we use … ?
a about anything we see
b only about something someone's wearing

c 💬 Say something nice about what your partner's wearing.

> I like your glasses. They look really good on you.
> Thanks!

6 PRONUNCIATION Connecting words

a ▶09.19 Listen to the sentences. Notice the words in **bold**. Is there a pause between them?

1 **Can I** help you?
2 What **size are** you?
3 Can I try **them on**?
4 How **much are** they?
5 The fitting rooms **are over** there.

b Notice how the words in **bold** in 6a are connected. The consonant sound moves to the start of the next word:

1 Can I ➔ Ca ni
2 size are ➔ si zare
3 them on ➔ the mon
4 much are ➔ mu chare
5 are over ➔ a **r**over

c 💬 In pairs, take turns saying the sentences in 6a and giving a reply. Try to link the words in **bold**.

> Can I help you?
> Yes, I'm looking for a coat.

7 SPEAKING

a Look at this dialogue map. Take notes about what you want to say.

Salesperson	Customer
Offer to help.	You want some jeans.
Size? Color?	Reply.
Show some jeans.	Ask to try them on.
Say they look great!	Ask how much.
Say the price.	Buy them. Credit card?

b 💬 Work in pairs. Use the dialogue map and your notes in 7a to make a conversation in a clothing store. Take turns being the salesperson and customer.

c 💬 In pairs, practice conversations like the one in 7a, but with different clothes. Take turns being the salesperson and customer.

✓ UNIT PROGRESS TEST

➔ CHECK YOUR PROGRESS

You can now do the **Unit Progress Test**.

1 LISTENING AND SPEAKING

a 💬 Look at the picture and answer the questions with a partner.

1 What kinds of presents do you like to get?
2 What kinds don't you like? Why?

b ▶09.20 What kinds of presents do you give your family and friends? Do you think you are more like Brendan, Bob, Fernanda, or Leila? Listen and check.

1

Brendan

I always give my girlfriend an expensive birthday present.

2 **Bob**

We don't buy presents.

3 **Fernanda**

We buy small presents for the children.

4 **Leila**

I usually buy my husband a book or a movie.

c ▶09.20 Who are these sentences about? Listen again to check.

1 They always buy their own presents.
   Bob's children
2 He likes to read.
   _____
3 They don't get expensive presents.
   _____
4 She loves expensive presents.
   _____
5 They go out to eat on birthdays.
   _____

d 💬 Talk about the questions.

1 Who do you give presents to?
   • a child in your family
   • someone you visit
   • grandparents
   • someone who is sick in the hospital
   • a coworker

2 How do you thank people for presents?
   • write an email
   • send a text
   • write a letter
   • call

2 READING

a It was Brendan's 30th birthday last week, and Molly gave him a present. Complete a–e in his thank-you email with sentences 1–5.

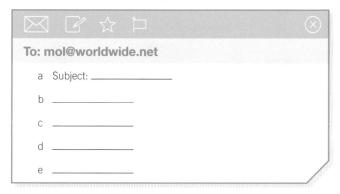

To: mol@worldwide.net

a Subject: _____

b _____

c _____

d _____

e _____

1 Hi, Molly.
2 Love, Brendan
3 Thanks very much for the movie theater tickets. They're a really great present!
4 Birthday present
5 There's a movie I want to see, so I'll use them this weekend.

b Read the email in 2a again. Answer the questions.

1 Who is Molly?
   a Brendan's sister   b a coworker
2 How do you know?

c Read Molly's email to Mr. Lewis and answer the questions.

1 Who is Mr. Lewis?
   a someone she worked with   b a friend
2 Why did he give her a present?
   a It's her birthday.   b She's leaving the company.

d Read Molly's email again. Answer the questions.

1 How is her email different from Brendan's email in 2a? Think about:
   • how she begins
   • how she ends
   • how she says thank you
2 Why do you think it's different?

Subject: Thank you

Dear Mr. Lewis,

I just want to say thank you very much for the book you gave me on my last day. It's a very nice present.

I really enjoyed working for you, and I wish you all the best.

Regards,

Molly

Molly

3 WRITING SKILLS
Writing formal and informal emails

a Sentences 1–4 all say thank you. Add one word to each sentence to make it correct.

you
¹Thank for the nice present.

²I'd just like to say thank you very for the beautiful flowers.

³Thanks so for the chocolates. They're delicious!

⁴Thank you the socks. They're a beautiful color.

b Which sentence in 3a is more formal than the others?

c Which of these phrases can you use in an email to someone you know well (1) or to someone you don't know well (2)?

Beginning
☐ Hello, Mrs. Finch.
☐ Hi there!
☐ Hi Marie,
☐ Dear Mr. Parker,

Ending
☐ Love,
☐ Thanks,
☐ Best wishes,
☐ Regards,
☐ See you,

4 WRITING

a Think of a present for someone in the class. Write the word on a piece of paper, then give them the "present."

chocolates

b Plan a thank-you email for the present.
Think of:
   • how to begin the email
   • how to end the email
   • what to say about the present.

c Write your email. Use the email in 2a to help you.

d 💬 Switch emails with another student and check:
☐ the beginning
☐ the sentence saying thank you
☐ the ending

e Write another email to someone you don't know well. What's different about it?

UNIT 9
Review and extension

1 GRAMMAR

a Write questions and answers for the people in the picture.

1 *What's he doing?   He's listening to music.*

b Complete the conversation with the correct form of the present continuous or simple present.

SHARON Hi, Jason. How are you? What ^{1}_____ (do)?
JASON Right now I ^{2}_____ (cook) dinner.
SHARON Really? But you never ^{3}_____ (cook).
JASON Well, I'm kind of bored with the food at the school cafeteria. I ^{4}_____ (make) spaghetti with tomato sauce.
SHARON Great. Usually when I ^{5}_____ (make) it, I ^{6}_____ (put) in a lot of pepper.
JASON Pepper? OK, I ^{7}_____ (add) it now.
SHARON But not too much. Jason? Jason? What's that noise? Are you there?
JASON Sorry, I dropped the phone. I ^{8}_____ (try) to cook and talk to you at the same time.

2 VOCABULARY

a Read the sentences. Which place in a shopping mall is it?

1 Not feeling too well? We can help!
2 Come see us when you want something new to wear!
3 Feeling hungry? Try our cheeseburgers!
4 Read the best new books!
5 We have 20 kinds of tea!
6 We have everything for your home!

b Write the correct clothes word under each picture.

1    2   3
_____   _____   _____

4   5    6
_____   _____   _____

3 WORDPOWER *time*

a Look at the phrases in **bold** in sentences 1–5. Match the phrases with meanings a–e.

1 You can **save time** by shopping online.
2 **It takes time** to learn a second language.
3 I'd like to work less so I can **spend time** with my family.
4 How do you **find time** to take care of four children and work?
5 She always **wastes time** playing computer games when she really needs to study.

a have time together with people
b do things in a short amount of time
c use time badly
d you need a lot of time
e have enough time

b Read the conversations. <u>Underline</u> the adjectives that you can change with *extra* and *good*.

1 **A** See you later. I'm on my way to the movies.
  B OK. Have a nice time.
2 **A** What do you like doing in your free time?
  B I really love reading.

c Complete the sentences with your own ideas.

1 It takes time to …
2 I save time by …
3 I can never find the time to …
4 I had a good time when I …
5 I sometimes waste time when I …

d 💬 Tell a partner your sentences in 3d. How similar are you?

⟳ REVIEW YOUR PROGRESS

How well did you do in this unit? Write 3, 2, or 1 for each objective.
3 = very well   2 = well   1 = not so well

I CAN ...	
Say where I am and what I'm doing	☐
Talk about the clothes I wear at different times	☐
Shop for clothes	☐
Write a thank-you email	☐

CAN DO OBJECTIVES

- Compare and talk about things you have
- Talk about languages
- Ask for help
- Write a post expressing an opinion

UNIT 10

COMMUNICATION

GETTING STARTED

a 💬 Look at the picture and answer the questions.

1 Who do you think these people are? Where are they?
2 Who are the children talking to?
3 What are the man and woman thinking?
4 What happened before this picture? What happens later?

b 💬 Which sentences are true for you?

1 I always have my cell phone with me.
2 If someone calls me, I always talk to them.
3 I never call people during meals.
4 I have my phone beside me when I sleep.

THEY'RE MORE COMFORTABLE THAN EARBUDS

1 READING

a 💬 Ask and answer the questions.

1 Where do you listen to music and/or podcasts?
2 How do you listen?

b Read the posts about using headphones or earbuds. Who talks about … ?

1 cost _____
2 sound quality _____
3 size _____
4 where to use them _____

c Read the posts again. Answer the questions.

1 How does Alyssa carry her earbuds?
2 How does Pedro carry his headphones?
3 Why does Kyle feel OK about spending money?
4 Why doesn't Emily want to spend a lot of money?
5 Where does Monica use her earbuds?
6 How does Noah carry his headphones?
7 Why is the sound on headphones clear?
8 What's Noah's problem with earbuds?

d 💬 Ask and answer the questions.

1 Do you prefer earbuds or headphones? Why?
2 What problems can you have when you use earbuds or headphones?

headphones

earbuds

Lifestyle Chat ☰

How do you like listening to music? Over-ear headphones or earbuds? Tell us what you prefer, and don't forget to vote!

Alyssa Yesterday
Earbuds are better than headphones. They are nice and small, and they fit in my pocket. Headphones are too big!

Pedro Yesterday
Well, yeah, headphones are bigger than earbuds, but headphones aren't that big. Mine fold up and go in my bag, no problem!

Kyle Yesterday
Most headphones are more expensive than earbuds, but I don't mind paying more for good sound.

Emily Yesterday
I do mind! I lose things all the time. If you're like me, it's better to buy something that's cheaper!

Monica Yesterday
Because they're smaller and lighter, you can use earbuds anywhere. I go to the gym, and I always take my earbuds with me. Headphones aren't very comfortable if you're working out!

Noah Yesterday
Some people say you can only use headphones at home, but I take mine everywhere – around town, when I'm traveling. They're more comfortable than earbuds, and my headphones come with a case – that makes them easy to carry.

Kyle 6 minute
Headphones – absolutely. There's no question!

Monica 5 minute
Well, I find the sound is clearer on headphones because they cover your ears. But if you buy a really good pair of earbuds – well, the sound is pretty good.

Noah 2 minute
I have really small ears, so earbuds always fall out! If you want comfort and great sound quality, then headphones are definitely better.

Alyssa 1 minute
They're smaller, cheaper, easier to use, and the sound quality is fine. I vote for earbuds – a winner for me in all categories.

2 GRAMMAR Comparative adjectives

a Underline the comparative adjectives in each sentence. Then circle the correct words to complete the rule.

1 Earbuds are better than headphones.
2 Headphones are bigger than earbuds.
3 Most headphones are more expensive than earbuds.
4 They're smaller, cheaper, easier to use.

The adjectives tell us how earbuds and headphones are *the same* / *different*.

b Underline more examples of comparative adjectives in the posts.

c Complete the rules about comparative adjectives.

1 Short adjectives (e.g., *small*) add _____
 hard → _____
2 Adjectives that end in -*y* (e.g., *easy*) change *y* to _____ and add _____
 happy → _____
3 Write _____ before long adjectives (e.g., *expensive*)
 interesting → _____ interesting
4 Some adjectives are irregular (e.g., *good*, *bad*)
 good → _____
 bad → _worse_

d ▶10.01 Complete the sentences. Listen and check your answers.

a My new headphones are more comfortable _____ the old ones I had.
b Some headphones are cheaper _____ earbuds.

e ▶10.01 **Pronunciation** Listen again. Is the missing word in 2d stressed or not?

f ≫ Now go to Grammar Focus 10A on p. 156.

g ≫ **Communication 10A** Student A go to p. 134. Student B go to p. 137.

3 LISTENING

a ▶10.03 Listen to Ruby talk to her father, Greg. Answer the questions.

Greg   Ruby

1 What does Greg want to change?
2 Does Ruby agree with him?

b ▶10.03 Listen again and put notes 1 to 4 in the correct place in the chart.

1 they cost more
2 you can forget to charge them
3 good in emergencies, like a storm
4 you can do many things with them

	good	*bad*
Landline phones		
Cell phones		

c 💬 Do you and people in your family still have a landline? Why / Why not?

4 VOCABULARY IT collocations

a Complete the phrases from the conversation with the correct verbs. Listen and check your answers.

1 g_ online   2 c_ _ _ _ my email   3 m_ _ _ calls

b Match verbs 1–6 with nouns a–f. Sometimes more than one answer is possible.

1 download
2 click on
3 visit
4 log into
5 save
6 charge

a a website
b a document
c a file
d a phone
e a link
f a computer

c 💬 Ask and answer questions using the phrases in 4a and 4b.

> How often do you check your email?

> What kind of websites do you visit?

> Do you use social media at work?

5 SPEAKING

a Choose idea 1 or 2.

1 something new you have compared to something old you had (e.g., smartphone / flip phone)
2 two things that you use and are similar (e.g., desktop computer / laptop computer)

b Take notes about the two things.

● Is one better than the other? How?
 bigger, easier to carry around, ...
● What can you do with each thing?
 go online, take photos, ...

c 💬 Talk about the two things. Ask each other questions.

> Are you happy with your new smartphone?

> Which do you think is better, your computer or your laptop?

10B WHAT'S THE MOST BEAUTIFUL LANGUAGE IN THE WORLD?

Learn to talk about languages

G Superlative adjectives
V High numbers

1 LISTENING

a 💬 Ask and answer the questions.

1 Which languages can you speak?
2 Which languages would you like to learn?
3 Look at the languages in the box. Where do people speak these languages?

Navajo ☐	Italian ☐	English ☐	French ☐
Arabic ☐	Quechua ☐	Japanese ☐	
Mandarin Chinese ☐	Portuguese ☐	Spanish ☐	

b ▶10.04 Listen to Professor Ryan Hunter talking about languages on the radio. Check (✓) the languages in 1a that he talks about.

c ▶10.04 Match sentences 1–4 with the languages Professor Hunter talks about. Listen and check your answers.

1 He thinks it's a very beautiful language.
2 It's a difficult language for English speakers, but not for Mandarin Chinese speakers.
3 Many people think it's very easy.
4 Over 900 million people speak it.

d ▶10.04 Listen again and answer the questions.

1 What was the first language Professor Hunter learned?
2 How many languages can he speak?
3 Where do people speak Navajo?
4 How much of the world's population speak Mandarin Chinese?

e 💬 Choose one thing Professor Hunter said which you think is ... .

a interesting   b surprising

2 GRAMMAR Superlative adjectives

a ▶10.05 Complete the sentences with the words in the box. Listen and check your answers.

best	easiest	musical	biggest	hardest

1 Mrs. Monti was the _____ teacher at my school.
2 Italian is the most _____ language I know.
3 The _____ language to learn is Navajo.
4 Spanish is the _____ language to learn.
5 China has the _____ population in the world.

b Read the sentences below and put the languages in order (1 = very easy, 4 = very difficult).

For me, **French** is easier than **Japanese**. But people say that **Spanish** is the easiest language in the world and **Navajo** is the most difficult.

c Think about your own language. What number do you think it has (1= very easy, 4 = very difficult)?

d Look at the sentences in 2a. Then complete the rules and the examples.

1 Short adjectives (e.g., *hard*) add _____
  small → _____
2 Write _____ before long adjectives (e.g., *musical*)
  expensive → _____
3 Some adjectives are irregular (e.g., *good*, *bad*)
  good → the _____
  bad → the worst

e ≫ Now go to Grammar Focus 10B on p. 156.

f ▶10.07 **Pronunciation** Listen to these phrases. Notice how the words are stressed.

the <u>bi</u>ggest   the <u>ea</u>siest   the <u>har</u>dest

g ▶10.08 **Pronunciation** Listen to these questions. Where's the main stress: on *most* or on the adjective?

What's the most beautiful language in the world?
What's the most useful language to speak?
What's the most difficult language in the world?

h 💬 Ask and answer the questions in 2g with other students.

Professor Hunter

3 READING

a 💬 Ask and answer the questions.

1 Do you read any blogs online? What are they about?
2 Do you use any language websites?
3 What do you think this blog is about?

b Read the blog post and check your answer to question 3 in 3a.

c Complete the blog post with the superlative forms of the adjectives in the box.

difficult (x2)   fast   heavy   big   long   popular   short
expensive   good

d Read the blog post again. Who or what are these people talking about?

1 "He could speak to people from many different countries."
2 "It's a very popular indigenous language."
3 "It takes a long time to learn the alphabet."
4 "I'd love to have this book, but it costs too much."
5 "She speaks too quickly! I can't understand her."
6 "I can say the words, but I never know how to write them correctly."

e 💬 Talk about the questions.

1 Which fact do you think is the most interesting? Why?
2 Do you know any other language facts?

4 VOCABULARY High numbers

a Find these numbers in 1c and the blog post. What do they refer to?

nine hundred million	
six hundred and three	
six hundred thousand	

b ≫ Now go to Vocabulary Focus 10B on p. 169 for more high numbers.

c 💬 Write down a high number for your partner to say.

5 SPEAKING

a Complete the questions with the superlative forms of the adjectives.

What or who is … ?

1 _____ (nice) word you know in English
2 _____ (beautiful) word in your language
3 _____ (good) language learner you know
4 _____ (long) word you can think of in your language
5 _____ (hard) word to pronounce in English
6 _____ (difficult) word to spell in your language
7 _____ (interesting) book you have

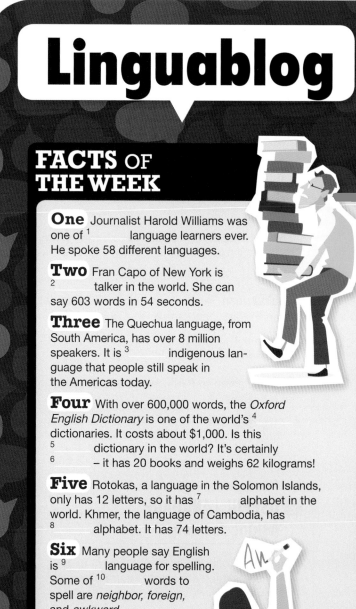

Linguablog

FACTS OF THE WEEK

One Journalist Harold Williams was one of [1] _____ language learners ever. He spoke 58 different languages.

Two Fran Capo of New York is [2] _____ talker in the world. She can say 603 words in 54 seconds.

Three The Quechua language, from South America, has over 8 million speakers. It is [3] _____ indigenous language that people still speak in the Americas today.

Four With over 600,000 words, the *Oxford English Dictionary* is one of the world's [4] _____ dictionaries. It costs about $1,000. Is this [5] _____ dictionary in the world? It's certainly [6] _____ – it has 20 books and weighs 62 kilograms!

Five Rotokas, a language in the Solomon Islands, only has 12 letters, so it has [7] _____ alphabet in the world. Khmer, the language of Cambodia, has [8] _____ alphabet. It has 74 letters.

Six Many people say English is [9] _____ language for spelling. Some of [10] _____ words to spell are *neighbor, foreign,* and *awkward.*

b 💬 Ask and answer the questions in 5a with other students.

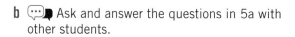

I think the nicest word in English is *elbow.* I like the sound of it.

Who is the best language learner you know?

10C EVERYDAY ENGLISH
There's something I don't know how to do

Learn to ask for help
- **S** Checking instructions
- **P** Main stress and intonation

1 LISTENING

a 💬 Ask and answer the questions.

1 Are you good at learning how to use new things? Why / Why not?
2 You have a problem with something that you can't fix. What do you do? Why?
   a Read the instructions.
   b Ask someone in your family or a friend for help.
   c Take it back to the store for help.
   d Watch a video about it on the Internet.

b ▶10.10 Juan Pablo needs help with his tablet. Listen to Part 1 and answer the questions.

1 What problem does Juan Pablo have with his tablet?
2 What app is open on Juan Pablo's tablet?

c ▶10.10 Listen to Part 1 again and answer the questions.

1 How does Hana feel about helping Juan Pablo?
2 Why does Juan Pablo want to put his tablet on silent?

2 USEFUL LANGUAGE
Asking for help

a ▶10.11 Look at the different ways to ask for help. Which ones does Juan Pablo use? Listen and check your answers.

1 Could you help me?
2 Can you help me?
3 Would you mind showing me?
4 Do you mind showing me?

b ▶10.12 Check (✓) the correct sentences. Correct the wrong sentences. Listen and check your answers.

1 ☐ Can you explain that?
2 ☐ Would you mind tell me?
3 ☐ Do you mind explaining it to me?
4 ☐ Could you showing me?
5 ☐ Would you mind helping me?

c Match the questions with the correct answers. One answer is correct for both questions.

1 Could you help me?
2 Do you mind helping me?

a No problem.
b Yes, of course.
c No, not at all.

3 PRONUNCIATION
Main stress and intonation

a ▶10.11 Listen for the question below and notice the main stress.

Do you mind <u>showing</u> me?

b What kind of word has the main stress when we ask for help?

c ▶10.11 Listen again. Does the intonation go up ↗ or down ↘?

d 💬 In pairs, practice saying the sentences in 2b and 3a.

e Think of a small problem you have with studying English. Think of a question to ask your partner for help.

f 💬 Take turns practicing asking for help and agreeing to help each other. Use questions from 2a.

> I don't understand this word. Would you mind explaining it to me?

> No problem.

4 LISTENING

a ▶10.13 Listen to Part 2 and answer the questions.

1 Does Hana help Juan Pablo with his problem?
2 Does Juan Pablo learn how to solve the problem?

b ▶10.13 Listen to Part 2 again. Hana tells Juan Pablo to do these things. Put them in the correct order.

a ☐ Open a new screen.
b ☐ Touch this icon.
c ☐ Move the slider.
d ☐ Touch the "Yes" box.

5 CONVERSATION SKILLS
Checking instructions

a Look at the sentences from the conversation. Who says them: Hana (*H*) or Juan Pablo (*JP*)?

1 **So first** I touch this icon?
2 I open this screen. **Is that right**?
3 I move the slider **like this**?

b Why does Juan Pablo ask these questions?

a He wants to be sure he understands the instructions.
b He wants Hana to repeat the instructions.

c Look at the the words in **bold** in 5a. Which expression does Juan Pablo use when he's doing something?

d Put the instructions in the correct order.

a ☐ And next, go to a new screen.
b ☐ And last, save the photos here.
c ☐ Touch the word "Open" here.

e In pairs, take turns practicing giving and checking instructions. Use the instructions in 5d and these phrases. There is no correct answer.

So first   Is that right?   Like this?

> Touch the word "Open" here.

> So first I touch the word "Open"?

6 SPEAKING

a ≫ **Communication 10C** Student A look at the information below. Student B go to p. 136.

Conversation 1. Read your first card. Think about what you want to say. Then start the conversation with Student B.

① You bought a new phone, but you can't receive text messages on it. Ask Student B for help. Check the instructions he/she gives you.

b **Conversation 2.** Now look at your second card. Think about what you want to say. Then listen to Student B and reply.

② Student B bought a new mouse for his/her computer, but it isn't working. When he/she asks for help, explain how the mouse works. Here are the instructions:

• Turn on the mouse and wait for the green light.
• Double click on the mouse.
• Wait ten seconds and click again. The mouse is working now.

✓ UNIT PROGRESS TEST

→ CHECK YOUR PROGRESS

You can now do the Unit Progress Test.

10D SKILLS FOR WRITING
My friends send really funny texts

Learn to write a post expressing an opinion

W Linking ideas with *also*, *too*, and *as well*

1 SPEAKING AND LISTENING

a 💬🎙 Ask and answer the questions.

1 Do you send messages on your phone and on social media?
2 If you do, when do you send them?
   - on vacation
   - when you're traveling
   - at work
   - when you go out
   Why do you send them?
3 If not, why not? How do you contact people?

b Match messages a–d with pictures 1–4. Where are the people and what are they doing?

c ▶10.14 Listen to three people talking about text messages. Which of texts a–d do you think they sent?

d ▶10.14 Listen again and complete the chart.

	Sends texts to	Prefers to	Why?
Speaker 1			
Speaker 2			
Speaker 3			

e 💬🎙 Which speaker's opinion is most similar to yours? In what way?

a Takeoff not till 7:30, so home later than I thought. Maybe around 10. I'll text again when we land. xx

b Here's a pic of our first meal in Italy!

c Hungry! Anything for dinner? Train gets in 6:35. See you in a bit ;-)
Delivered

d Where are you? We're by the fountain. Can't see you.

2 READING

a Read the posts on the online discussion board. Check (✓) who sometimes get annoyed by people who use their phones.

☐ Genji   ☐ MadMax   ☐ Lars2
☐ Meepe   ☐ AdamB   ☐ Rainbows

b Read the posts again. Who thinks these things?

> ¹I don't know anyone without a smartphone.

> ²It can be fun to send texts to friends.

> ³People shouldn't send texts when they're eating with other people.

> ⁴It's rude not to look at someone when they're talking to you.

> ⁵I don't like people who post photos in the middle of a conversation.

c Underline all the adjectives in the posts. Which three are negative?

d Look at the posts again and find ... .
1 two ways to agree
2 one way to disagree

Things I **hate!**

Genji
I hate it when people look at their phone when they're talking to you. If you're talking to somebody, they should look at you, not at their phone. It's the worst thing you can do if you're with someone. I have a friend who does that.

Meepe
Yes, I agree. I also have a friend like that. You're talking to him, and he starts scrolling on his phone! It's so annoying.

MadMax
Yes, you're right, it's really rude. Some people post on social media in the middle of a conversation as well. I hate that.

AdamB
Yes, my sister does that, too. We're having dinner, and she starts sending texts to all her friends. I text my friends a lot, too, but I try to put my phone down during dinner.

Lars2
Sometimes that's annoying, but I can also understand why people do it. Sometimes I want to send an important text before I forget about it. Everyone has a smartphone these days. We all use our phones for everything!

Rainbows
I don't agree with you, Genji. I don't mind when my friends are on their phones. Messaging is useful if you want to meet a friend. Also, my friends send really funny texts, so we laugh a lot.

3 WRITING SKILLS
Linking ideas with *also*, *too*, and *as well*

a Look at the sentences and answer the question.

LARS2   Sometimes that's annoying, but I can also understand why people do it.

MEEPE   I also have a friend like that.

RAINBOWS   Messaging is useful if you want to meet a friend. Also, my friends send really funny texts.

Where does the word *also* come in each sentence? Underline the correct answer.
1 *before* / *after* an auxiliary verb (*be, can* …)
2 *before* / *after* a main verb (*get, send, live* …)
3 at the *beginning* / *end* of a new sentence.

b Look at the sentences below and underline words or phrases that mean the same as *also*. Then answer the question.

1 **ADAMB**   Yes, my sister does that, too.
2 **MADMAX**   Some people post on social media in the middle of a conversation as well.

Where do they come in the sentence: at the beginning, in the middle, or at the end?

c Add *also*, *too*, or *as well* to these sentences.
1 I have a new PC, and I have a new laptop.
2 We had GPS on our smartphones, and we took a street map.
3 She works for a cell phone company, and she knows a lot about computers.
4 Tablets are very light to carry. They have a large screen, so they are easy to read.

4 WRITING AND SPEAKING

a Plan a post about something that annoys you. Use these ideas or your own. Take notes.
- another form of technology (not phones)
- people's bad habits
- an activity you hate doing

b Write your post. Use the ones on the discussion board to help you. Give your post to another student.

c Agree or disagree with another student's post, and try to add a sentence with *also*, *too*, or *as well*. Then pass your post to the next student.

d Check the linking words in other students' posts. Did they use *also*, *too*, and *as well* correctly?

e 💬 Compare posts. Which do you think is the most interesting? Why?

UNIT 10
Review and extension

1 GRAMMAR

a Complete the conversation with the comparative forms of the adjectives in parentheses.

NEIL Which laptop is ¹ _better_ (good)?

ASSISTANT Well, the Alba is ² _____ (powerful) than the Plexus; it has 16 gigabytes of RAM. It also has a ³ _____ (big) screen. But it's ⁴ _____ (expensive) than the Plexus – it's $1,000 more.

NEIL Which one is ⁵ _____ (heavy)? The Alba?

ASSISTANT Yes. The Plexus is ⁶ _____ (light) and ⁷ _____ (thin) than the Alba. So the Plexus is a ⁸ _____ (practical) laptop if you're traveling. And it's a little ⁹ _____ (fast) than the Alba, too.

b Complete the questions with one word from each box. Use the superlative form of the adjectives.

> long   big   expensive   hot   good

> soccer player   country   hotel room   river   place

1   **A**   What's ª _____ in the world?
    B   Death Valley in California. The highest temperature was 56°C.
2   **A**   What's ᵇ _____ in Africa?
    B   The Nile. It's 6,695 kilometers long.
3   **A**   What's ᶜ _____ in the world?
    B   One in the President Wilson Hotel in Geneva. It costs $80,000 for one night.
4   **A**   Who's ᵈ _____ ever?
    B   Many people say it's Pelé from Brazil. He scored over 1,000 goals and won the World Cup three times.
5   **A**   What's ᵉ _____ in the world?
    B   That's easy – Russia. It's 17 million km².

2 VOCABULARY

a Underline the correct words.

1   Don't forget to *click on / save* the document when you close it. You don't want to lose it.
2   He *visits / goes* online for hours every evening. He just goes from one *document / website* to the next.
3   How can I *log into / click on* your computer? I want to *visit / check* my email.
4   *Click on / Visit* this link to download the *file / computer*.

b Write the numbers as words.

1 50,000,000	3 256	5 200,000
2 2003	4 1,500	6 2,655

3 WORDPOWER *most*

a Read the text and answer the questions.

1   Which four languages does the family speak?
2   Which language does the writer prefer speaking? Which does her mother prefer speaking? Why?

One family – four languages

My mother is Mexican, my father is from Germany, we spent ten years in England, and now we live in Brazil. So we speak four languages in our family!

¹**Most** of the people we know here are Brazilian, so when people come to our house, we speak Portuguese ²**most** of the time, but ³**most** of them understand English, too, so we sometimes speak English and Portuguese together. I like speaking English ⁴**most** of all because I went to school in London and also because it's an international language and ⁵**most** people speak it. But with my parents, I usually speak Spanish or German. My mother always prefers to speak Spanish with us – she says it's ⁶**the most** beautiful language in the world.

b Look at the phrases with *most* in the text in 3a. Which of phrases 1–6 mean ... ?

a   more than all the others
b   nearly all (or about 70–80%)

c Look at the phrases *most of the people* and *most people* in the text. Which is about ... ?

a   people in general
b   a particular group of people

d Complete the sentences with the words in the box.

> people   of the way
> of the evening   of my friends

1   I spent most _____ at a friend's house, then I went home.
2   Most _____ in the U.S. speak English, but there are also more than 40 million Spanish speakers.
3   It's a very nice walk. You go along a river most _____.
4   I'm nearly 70, and most _____ don't work now.

e Write two sentences about your life. Choose two phrases.

most of the time	most of all
most of my friends	most days

f 💬 Tell a partner your sentences and ask and answer questions. How similar are you?

UNIT 11

ENTERTAINMENT

GETTING STARTED

a 💬 Look at the picture and answer the questions.

1 What do you think these people are watching? Here are some ideas:
- a concert
- a movie
- a music video
- homemade videos

2 What do you like to watch with your friends? Do you like the same things?

b 💬 Talk about movies or TV shows you enjoyed when you were a child. Say why.

11A | I'VE HEARD SHE'S A GOOD ACTRESS

Learn to ask and answer about entertainment experiences

G Present perfect
V Irregular past participles

1 READING

a 💬📢 Look at the pictures of the three actresses. What do you think they have in common?

- a They went to the same school.
- b They all lived in Australia.
- c They were models before they became actresses.
- d They are married to movie directors.

b Read the fact files. Find the answer to 1a.

c 💬📢 Read the quiz questions about the actresses. Guess the answers.

d Read the article and find out the answers to the quiz.

e 💬📢 Talk about the questions.

1 Who do you think is the most interesting actress? Why?
2 Do you know any other famous Australian actors or actresses?

FILM International

International Movie Stars

Rose Byrne, Mia Wasikowska, and Margot Robbie are three famous actresses who work in Hollywood, and they have many things in common.

All three come from Australia, and before they went to Hollywood, their first acting jobs were in Australian TV dramas and soap operas. They've acted in some very popular movies and TV. Rose was in *Bridesmaids*, two *X-Men* movies, and the *Peter Rabbit* series of movies. Mia was in *Jane Eyre* and *Alice Through the Looking Glass*. Margot was in *The Legend of Tarzan; I, Tonya;* and *Mary Queen of Scots*. All three women have won awards in the U.S. and Australia for their acting.

However, they have done some interesting and unusual things away from the movie business. Rose has worked for UNICEF in Australia. She's also a model and has been in TV commercials for the makeup company Max Factor. Margot was in the movie *The Legend of Tarzan*. Before she started filming that movie, she learned to swing on a circus trapeze. She also learned to ice-skate to play Tonya Harding in the movie *I, Tonya*. Mia studied dance in school and has directed some short films. Now she really loves taking photos and won a national prize in Australia for one of her photos.

Rose, Mia, and Margot are not just three amazing actresses, they are three amazing women.

FACT FILE: MARGOT ROBBIE
Born   1990 Dalby, Australia
Childhood Australia
Lives   Los Angeles

FACT FILE: MIA WASIKOWSKA
Born   1989 Canberra, Australia
Childhood Australia & Poland
Lives   Sydney

THE QUIZ
Is **Hollywood** all they have **in common?**

Rose, Mia, and Margot have also done some interesting and unusual things that you might not know about. Try our quiz. Can you guess which actress has done these things?

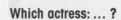

Which actress: … ?

1 has been in a makeup advertisement
2 can dance well
3 likes to use her camera a lot
4 can ice-skate well
5 has been in TV commercials
6 learned to swing on a circus trapeze

FACT FILE: ROSE BYRNE
Born   1979 Sydney, Australia
Childhood Australia
Lives   New York

2 GRAMMAR Present perfect: affirmative

a Complete the sentences. Check your answers in the article.

1 They _____ _____ in some very popular movies.
2 Rose _____ _____ for UNICEF in Australia.
3 Mia _____ _____ some short films.

b Do we know when in the past the actresses did these things?

c Complete the rule with the correct verb.

I / you / we / they + _____ ('ve)
he / she / it + _____ ('s)   + past participle (e.g., *worked*)

3 LISTENING

a ▶11.01 Maggie and Stephen answer the magazine quiz about the actresses. Listen and answer the questions.

1 Did they both guess all the correct answers?
2 Check (✓) the films they talk about:

a ☐ *Bridesmaids*   d ☐ *X-Men*
b ☐ *I, Tonya*   e ☐ *Jane Eyre*
c ☐ *Mary Queen of Scots* f ☐ *The Legend of Tarzan*

b ▶11.01 Listen again. Check (✓) if they've seen a movie this actress is in. Then write the letter (a–f) of the movie in 3a they've seen her in.

	Rose Byrne	Mia Wasikowska	Margot Robbie
Maggie			✓ b
Stephen			

c What did Maggie and Stephen think about the actresses in the movies they've seen?

4 VOCABULARY Irregular past participles

a ▶11.02 Complete the sentences from the conversation with the words in the box. Listen and check your answers.

heard   seen (x2)   read

1 I've never _____ any of Mia Wasikowska's movies.
2 I've _____ she's a good actress.
3 I've _____ the book, I but haven't _____ the movie.

Do the verbs end in *-ed*?

b ≫ Go to Vocabulary Focus 11A on p. 170.

5 GRAMMAR Present perfect: negative and questions

a ▶11.05 Complete the sentences from the conversation with the words in the box. Listen and check your answers.

ever   never   seen

1 I haven't _____ the movie.
2 I've _____ seen any of Mia Wasikowska's movies.
3 Have you _____ seen any of her movies?

b Complete the rules with the words *before* and *after*.

1 When we use *not*, *ever*, and *never*, they come _____ *have* in the present perfect.
2 When we make a question in the present perfect, *have* comes _____ the subject.

c ▶11.05 **Pronunciation** Listen again to the sentences in 5a. Do we stress *have* or the past participle?

d ≫ Now go to Grammar Focus 11A on p. 158.

e ▶11.07 Complete the conversation with the present perfect form of the verbs in parentheses. Listen and check your answers.

A ¹_____ (you/see) the movie *Crazy Rich Asians*?
B Yes, I have – it's so funny. What about you?
A I ²_____ (read) the book, but I ³_____ (not see) the movie. ⁴_____ (you/read) the book?
B No, I haven't, but I want to. I ⁵_____ (hear) that there are three books.
A That's right.
B ⁶_____ (they/make) movies of the other books?
A I'm not sure. I'll check online.

6 SPEAKING

a Think of some popular movies, TV shows, and books. Write six questions about these things. Look at the questions in 5e to help you.

b 💬 Ask other students your questions from 6a.

Have you watched *NCIS* on TV?

Yes, I like it.

No, I haven't. Is it a good show?

Learn to talk about events you've been to

G Present perfect or simple past
V Music

1 READING

a 💬 Look at picture a. What kind of dance are they doing?

b Look at *Buenos Aires: City of music*. Do you think it is about … ?

1 famous Argentinean bands
2 places to hear music
3 tango dancing

Read the text and check your ideas.

c Read the article again. Match pictures a–e with the places in the article.

d Read *Buenos Aires: City of music* again and answer the questions.

1 Which is the most expensive place to go?
2 Where can you hear more than one type of music?
3 What's the best time to go to *The Roxy*?
4 Which place(s) do you think are popular with both visitors and people who live in the city?

e 💬 You're in Buenos Aires. Choose one place you'd like to go to, and one place you wouldn't like to go to. Why / Why not?

Buenos Aires: City of Music

Did you know Buenos Aires is one of the world's best cities for music? And it isn't only tango orchestras you can hear. Whatever kind of music you like, you can find it somewhere – it's a city of restaurants, cafés, clubs, and music venues.

CLASSICAL MUSIC AND OPERA

It's easy to find good classical music in Buenos Aires. The best orchestras from all over the world play in the **Teatro Colón** and you can also see the most popular operas. It's not cheap, but you pay less if you get a ticket for a whole season.

JAZZ AND POP MUSIC

Buenos Aires is full of jazz clubs, but the most interesting is probably **Jazz y Pop**. It's in a tiny room in a basement, and the musicians play in the middle of the room. And not only jazz – they also play rock, pop, and folk music. Musicians come from all over the world to play there for free, so you might see someone famous!

Or if you like drums, visit the **Konex Cultural Center**. A band called *La Bomba de Tiempo* play drums there every Monday night. They play dance music from Africa and Latin America. Tourists and local people come together to enjoy the party and dance all night long.

Then there's **The Roxy**. It has a stage for live rock music and a room for dance music with DJs. Go there late – the bands don't start playing until 2 a.m., and the crowds start arriving around 3. Drinks are expensive!

TANGO IN THE STREET

Go to the **San Telmo** district. It's full of great cafés and shops – and also musicians and singers. On a warm summer evening, you can see tango dancers in the street. There's a space for dancing in every café. It's free, so bring your dancing shoes!

2 VOCABULARY Music

a ▶**11.08** Underline words in the text for … .

1 kinds of music: *tango*, …
2 people who play music, sing or dance:
   an orchestra, …

Listen and check your answers.

b ▶**11.09** **Pronunciation** Listen to these words again. Circle the number of syllables. Underline the stressed syllable in each word.

dancer   1 2 3   orchestra 1 2 3
musician 1 2 3   opera   1 2 3
classical 1 2 3

c ▶**11.10** Listen to five pieces of music. What kind of music are they?

d 💬 Which kinds of music do you often listen to? Which kinds do you never listen to?

3 LISTENING

a ▶**11.11** Max and Alana are students in Buenos Aires. Listen to their conversation about *Buenos Aires: City of Music.* How many places do they talk about? Which places have they been to?

b ▶**11.11** Complete the chart about Alana. Listen and check your answers.

Where?	When?	Did she like it?
1 *Jazz y Pop*		
2		
3		

4 GRAMMAR
Present perfect or simple past

a ▶**11.12** Match the questions with the answers. Listen and check your answers.

1 Have you ever been to *Jazz y Pop*?
  a Yes, I went there two weeks ago. They had a really good band.

2 What about *The Roxy*? Have you been there?
  b Yes, of course I have. We all went there for Antonia's birthday.

3 I bet you've never been to the *Teatro Colón*.
  c Yes, I have, actually. I went there last year.

b Answer the questions about 4a.

1 Which two tenses do the speakers use?
  a simple present   c present continuous
  b simple past   d present perfect
2 Which tense do we use … ?
  a if we don't say when something happened
  b if we say when something happened
3 Which tense do we use with … ?
  a *ever* and *never*
  b time expressions (*last weekend*, *a month ago*)

c ≫ Now go to Grammar Focus 11B on p. 158.

d ▶**11.14** Put the conversation in the correct order. Listen and check your answers.

A ☐ Who did you go with?
A ☐ I've heard that's a great festival! Did you enjoy it?
A [1] Have you ever been to a music festival?
A ☐ Where was it?
B ☐ It was in Rio de Janeiro – the Rock in Rio festival.
B ☐ I went with a group of friends from college.
B ☐ Yes, we all had a great time.
B ☐ Yes, I have. I went to one last summer.

e 💬 Practice the conversation in 4d.

5 SPEAKING

a Think of two things you've seen or places you've been to in your town or city. Here are some ideas:
  • a concert or music event
  • a movie or play
  • a theater, movie theater, or club

Take notes.

City Theater – Macbeth
football stadium – Rihanna concert

b Think of two things you haven't seen or places you haven't been to, but would like to. Take notes.

c 💬 Ask other students about the things and places in 5a and 5b. Ask for more information.

Have you been to Mombo's?   When did you go there?   Was it good?   Who did you go with?

11C EVERYDAY ENGLISH
I thought they were really good

1 LISTENING

a 💬🔊 Ask and answer the questions.

1 When you go out in the evening, do you ... ?
- drive • walk • take a bus • take a taxi • other
2 When was the last time you took a taxi? Where did you go?

b 💬🔊 Look at the picture. What are Paul and Celia doing?

c ▶11.15 Listen to Part 1 and check your answers in 1b. Then choose the correct answers below.

1 Paul and Celia are *going out / on their way home*.
2 Their address is *525 Washington Road / 255 Washington Road*.

d ▶11.15 Listen to Part 1 again and answer the questions.

1 Where have Paul and Celia been?
2 Do they have the same opinion about what they saw?

e ▶11.15 Read the sentences and write Paul (*P*), Celia (*C*), or both (*B*). Listen again to check your answers.

Who thinks ... ?

1 the concert was fun
2 not all the bands were good
3 Atlantis is a good band
4 Atlantis was too loud

2 USEFUL LANGUAGE
Asking for and expressing opinions

a ▶11.16 Listen and put the conversation in the correct order.

a ☐ Did you enjoy it?
b ☐ How about you?
c ☐ Yeah, me too.
d ☐ So what did you think of the concert?
e ☐ Yeah, it was okay.
f ☐ I had fun.

b 💬🔊 In pairs, practice the mini-conversation in 2a.

c Now look at these ways to express an opinion. Match opinions 1–3 with reasons a–c.

1 I really liked the first band.
2 I didn't like the first band very much.
3 I didn't like the first band at all.

a I thought they were terrible.
b I thought the singer was great.
c I thought they played pretty well, but their songs were boring.

b

3 LISTENING

a ▶ **11.17** What type of music do you like? Do you like to go to concerts? Look at the picture above. What type of music do you think the band is playing? Listen to Part 2 to check.

4 CONVERSATION SKILLS
Responding to an opinion

a Read the mini-conversations. Which replies mean … ?

    a I agree.   b I don't really agree.

1	**PAUL**	I didn't like the opening band.
	CELIA	No, me neither.
2	**CELIA**	I had fun. How about you?
	PAUL	Yeah, me too.
3	**PAUL**	I loved the last band.
	CELIA	You did?
4	**CELIA**	All their songs sound the same.
	PAUL	Do you think so?
5	**CELIA**	They were too loud.
	PAUL	Yeah, they were kind of loud.

b Complete the chart with *do* or *did*.

Present	Past
A I think they**'re** good.	**A** I thought they **were** good.
B You **do**?	**B** You ¹_____ ?
A Their music **is** interesting.	**A** The concert **was** boring.
B ²_____ you think so?	**B** **Did** you think so?

c 💬📢 In pairs, practice the mini-conversations in 4b. Take turns being A and B.

5 PRONUNCIATION
Main stress and intonation

a ▶ **11.18** Listen to these replies. Notice that both words are stressed in each one.

  1 You do? 2 You did? 3 Me neither. 4 Me too.

b ▶ **11.18** Listen again and answer the questions.

  1 Does the intonation go up ↗ or down ↘ at the end of each reply?
  2 In 1 and 2, do you think the speaker sounds … ?
    a angry   b surprised   c happy

c ▶ **11.18** Listen again and repeat.

d 💬📢 In pairs, take turns responding to these opinions. You can agree or disagree.

  1 I thought the concert was boring.
  2 I didn't enjoy the concert.
  3 I think the band plays very interesting music.
  4 I thought the concert was too long.
  5 I think she's a fantastic singer.

> You did? I thought it was really good.

6 LISTENING

a ▶ **11.17** Listen to Part 2 again. Are the sentences true or false? Correct the false sentences.

  1 Paul thinks Atlantis is a boring band.
  2 Paul wants to listen to music by Atlantis on his phone.
  3 Celia wants to hear Paul sing.
  4 Celia doesn't like pop music.
  5 Celia thinks Atlantis was too quiet.

7 SPEAKING

a ≫ **Communication 11C** Student A go to p. 134. Student B go to p. 136.

☑ UNIT PROGRESS TEST

➡ CHECK YOUR PROGRESS

You can now do the Unit Progress Test.

11D | SKILLS FOR WRITING
It was an interesting movie

1 SPEAKING AND LISTENING

a 💬 Look at the pictures on page 117. Ask and answer the questions.

1 Can you name the actors and the director?
2 Which movies are they famous for?
3 Have you seen any of their movies? Which one(s)?

b ▶11.19 Melissa and Ron talk about a movie. Listen and answer the questions.

1 What movie are they talking about?
2 Did Ron like it? Did Melissa like it?

c ▶11.19 Listen again. Write Ron (*R*) or Melissa (*M*). Who … ?

1 thinks James Bond movies are always the same
2 thinks James Bond movies are just for fun
3 thinks the special effects were good
4 is going to see the movies again

d Choose a movie you've seen and a movie you haven't seen. Take notes. Think of … .

• why you liked or didn't like the movie
• why you'd like to see the other movie

e 💬 Talk about the two movies from 1d.

1 Have other students seen them?
2 What did they think of them?

2 READING

a Ashley watched the movie *Roma*. Read her review. Is it positive or negative?

b Read Ashley's review again and answer the questions.

1 How many times has she watched the movie?
2 What are two things she says about Alfonso Cuarón?
3 What are two things she says about Yalitza Aparicio?

c Oscar also watched *Roma*. Read his review. Is it positive or negative?

d Read Oscar's review again and answer the questions.

1 Why did he watch it?
2 What are the good and bad things he says about the movie?

e Anna also watched *Roma*. Read her review. Is it positive or negative?

f Read Anna's review again and answer the questions.

1 Where did she watch it?
2 What new information does she give about the movie?

3 WRITING SKILLS Structuring a review

a Read Ashley's and Oscar's reviews again. Write the numbers of the sentences that answer the questions below.

a ☐4☐ Who are the actors and are they good?
b ☐ When did you see the movie?
c ☐ Did you like it?
d ☐ Do you recommend it?
e ☐ Who wrote or directed it?
f ☐ What is the movie about?

b Read Anna's review again. Does it answer the questions in the same order?

c Look at some comments about different movies. Which questions in 3a do they answer?

1 I loved it!
2 I heard it was good, so I went to see it on the weekend.
3 I thought the story was pretty interesting.
4 Emma Stone is amazing.
5 It's by American director Anthony Russo.
6 Don't go to see it. It's terrible!
7 I thought it was a funny movie. I laughed a lot.
8 The movie is about a boy who grows up in a small town in Texas.

ROMA

"I thought it was an interesting and very beautiful movie. So try to see it if you can."

Ashley

¹I saw *Roma* at the movies a month ago, and then I watched it again on Netflix. ²So I've watched it twice now, and it was even better the second time. ³It's by the Mexican director Alfonso Cuarón, and it's based on his own childhood growing up in Mexico City. ⁴All the actors are excellent, but I liked Yalitza Aparicio the best. She was completely unknown when Cuarón gave her the part, but she's great. ⁵She plays the role of a maid who works for a middle-class family, and the movie is the story of her relationship with the parents and the children of the family. ⁶I thought it was an interesting and very beautiful movie. So try to see it if you can.

d Look at the reviews again. How are sentences 1–3 different from the ones in the reviews?

1 I watched *Roma* on Netflix a few weeks ago. A friend recommended *Roma*, and we usually like the same movies, so I decided to watch *Roma*.

2 I liked Yalitza Aparicio the best. Yalitza Aparicio was completely unknown when Cuarón gave Yalitza Aparicio the part, but Yalitza Aparicio is great.

3 So I didn't think the movie was a great movie, but maybe it's OK to watch the movie if you have nothing better to do.

e 💬 Answer the questions with a partner.

1 How many times did the three people write the name of the movie in their reviews?

2 What words did they use in place of the name of the movie?

4 WRITING AND SPEAKING

a Plan a review of a movie you've seen. Take notes using the questions in 3a and the comments in 3b to help you.

b Write your review. Use Ashley's, Oscar's, and Anna's reviews to help you.

c Switch reviews with another student and check. Does your partner's review answer the questions in 3a?

d 💬 Read other students' reviews. Which movie would you like to see?

"OK to watch it if you have nothing to do one evening."

Oscar

[1]I watched *Roma* on Netflix a few weeks ago. [2]A friend recommended it, and we usually like the same movies, so I decided to watch it, but I was disappointed. [3]Alfonso Cuarón, who also made the movie *Gravity*, wrote and directed it. [4]The acting was good (Marina de Tavira is great in the role of the mother), but I found the story kind of boring. [5]The movie is about a family and their maid. All the characters in the movie just do ordinary things, and nothing exciting happens. [6]So I didn't think it was a great movie, but maybe it's OK to watch it if you have nothing better to do.

"A very interesting movie, but it was also very sad."

Anna

[1]I watched *Roma* at a friend's house last week. [2]I thought it was a very interesting movie, but it was also very sad, and the end of the movie made me cry. [3]The movie is by the Mexican director Alfonso Cuarón, and it's in black and white. [4]The movie is about a family in Mexico City and their life with their maid, who comes from a village. [5]The acting is very good, especially the actresses who play the maid and the mother. [6]I can recommend this movie, but only watch it if you enjoy sad movies!

UNIT 11
Review and extension

1 VOCABULARY

a Underline the correct words.

1 I don't like *classic* / *classical* music.
2 He likes old *rock* / *rocker* music like the Rolling Stones.
3 After years of playing the violin, he finally got a job with an *orchestral* / *orchestra*.
4 In my opinion, Lady Gaga is the most famous *popular* / *pop* music singer in the world.
5 Bill only plays his guitar on the street for money. But listen to him – he's a very good *musician* / *musical*.
6 Would you like to come and see *Così fan tutte*? It's a very famous *opera* / *operatic* by Mozart.

b Write the past participle of the verbs.

1	be	5	read
2	do	6	see
3	go	7	win
4	hear	8	write

2 GRAMMAR

a Write sentences and questions with the correct form of the present perfect.

1 I / be to South Africa twice.
2 She / meet a lot of famous actors.
3 you / see the latest James Bond movie?
4 He / not / work in an office before.
5 We / never / win the lottery.
6 they / read all the Harry Potter books?
7 I / not / hear a lot of jazz music.

b Check (✓) the correct sentences. Change the verb form in the sentences that are not correct.

1 We've been to Brazil only once.
2 He's read a book in English last week.
3 I never saw an *X-Men* movie.
4 They've won a pop music competition two years ago.
5 I saw three movies last weekend.
6 She's never been to Argentina.
7 I didn't read a book by Dan Brown.

c Complete the conversation with the correct present perfect or simple past form of the verbs in parentheses.

A ^{1}_____ (you/be) to Australia?
B No, I haven't, but I ^{2}_____ (be) to New Zealand.
A You have? I ^{3}_____ (never/be) there, but I would love to go.
B We ^{4}_____ (go) about four years ago in the summer.
A How long ^{5}_____ (you/stay)?
B About three weeks, but it ^{6}_____ (not be) long enough.
I ^{7}_____ (do) a bungee jump when I ^{8}_____ (be) there.
^{9}_____ (you/ever/try) anything like that?
A No. I'm too afraid!

3 WORDPOWER Multi-word verbs

a Match 1–6 with a–f to make conversations.

1 Sorry, Mike, I have a meeting now.
2 Here's my photo ID.
3 Are you from London?
4 Here's a very nice shirt in blue.
5 You're looking a little tired.
6 I have nothing to do this evening.

a Yes, I think I need to **lie down** for a while.
b Well, I was born in Manchester, but I **grew up** here.
c That's OK. I can **call** you **back** this afternoon.
d Well, would you like to **come over** for dinner?
e Thank you. Now can you **fill** this form **out**, please?
f Could I **try** it **on**?

b Match the multi-word verbs in **bold** in 3a with meanings 1–6.

1 return a phone call
2 put on clothes to check that the size is right
3 complete
4 take a rest on a sofa or bed
5 visit a person's home
6 go from being a child to an adult

c Complete the sentences with the correct form of a multi-word verb from 3a.

1 She never wants to _____ things _____ in the store and often gets the wrong size.
2 You need this form at the airport. Can you _____ it _____ before boarding the train?
3 I've always lived in Toronto. I _____ _____ here.
4 She finally _____ me _____ this morning and told me she was away all last week.
5 Why don't you _____ _____ and read your book?
6 My brother _____ _____ last night and brought a cake for my birthday.

d 💬 Work in pairs. Ask and answer the questions.

1 How often do friends or family come over to your place?
2 Do you sometimes forget to call people back?
3 Where did you grow up?
4 Do you usually try on clothes before you buy them?
5 What was the last form you had to fill out?
6 Do you sometimes lie down during the day?

⟳ REVIEW YOUR PROGRESS

How well did you do in this unit? Write 3, 2, or 1 for each objective.
3 = very well   2 = well   1 = not so well

I CAN ...	
ask and answer about entertainment experiences	☐
talk about events I've been to	☐
express opinions about things I've seen	☐
write a review	☐

CAN DO OBJECTIVES

- Talk about vacation plans
- Give advice about traveling
- Use language for travel and tourism
- Write an email with travel advice

UNIT 12

TRAVEL

GETTING STARTED

a 💬📢 Look at the picture and answer the questions.

1 Where do you think this man is on vacation? Why?
2 What other things has he planned to do there?
3 Who do you think took this picture?

b 💬📢 In pairs, ask and answer the questions.

1 Do you take photos of friends and family on vacations or other special days?
2 What other things do you photograph?
3 What do you do with your photos after you've taken them?
4 What's your favorite photograph?

12A | WHAT ARE YOU GOING TO DO?

1 VOCABULARY Geography

a Match words 1–10 with pictures a–j.

1	island	6	desert
2	mountain	7	lake
3	forest	8	glacier
4	waterfall	9	rainforest
5	beach	10	river

b ▶ **12.01** **Pronunciation** Listen and check your answers in 1a. Then answer the questions.

1 Which two words have only one syllable?
2 Which syllable is stressed in all the other words?

c 💬 Work in pairs. Look at pictures a–j and answer the questions.

1 Which places would you like to live near?
2 Have you been to any of these places?
3 Which place would you like to go to on vacation? Why?

d ≫ Now go to Vocabulary Focus 12A on p. 170 for more geography vocabulary.

2 READING

a 💬 What's important for you when you're on vacation? Why?

- nothing – just relax
- meet new people
- do a lot of sightseeing
- understand a new culture
- try a new sport
- eat local food

b Read the web page. Which ideas in 2a can you do on Work Around the World vacations?

c Read the web page again. What is a good job for someone who likes … ?

- swimming and dancing
- drawing
- outdoor sports

d 💬 Talk about the questions.

1 Would you like to do one of these jobs? Why / Why not?
2 Order the three jobs from hard work (1) to not very hard work (3). Say why.

WORK AROUND THE WORLD

What are Work Around the World vacations?

They're vacations where you work for a few hours every day, and you get your accommodations and food free.

Why go on a Work Around the World vacation?

Because it's fun, you help other people, and you also make a lot of interesting new friends.

Here are some examples of great Work Around the World vacations.

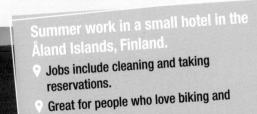

Summer work in a small hotel in the Åland Islands, Finland.

📍 Jobs include cleaning and taking reservations.

📍 Great for people who love biking and kayaking.

3 LISTENING

a ▶ **12.03** Listen to two conversations about vacation plans. Which Work Around the World vacations are Emily and Chloe interested in?

b ▶ **12.03** Listen again to the two conversations. Answer the questions.

Conversation 1
1 Why doesn't Emily want to go to college?
2 What does she like about the job she is interested in?
3 Why doesn't Zoe want her to go?

Conversation 2
1 Why does Chloe want to quit her job?
2 What does she like about the job she is interested in?
3 Does Frank think it's a good job for Chloe?

c 💬🗣 Talk about the questions.
1 Do you think it's a good idea for Emily and Chloe to do a Work Around the World vacation? Why / Why not?
2 What are the good things and the bad things about going on one of these vacations?

A Mexican family is looking for a young person to work in their home in Acapulco on the Pacific Coast.
📍 Jobs include taking care of children and teaching English.
📍 Great for people who love cycling and dancing.

Come and live in an artists' town in the South Island of New Zealand.
📍 Jobs include helping in the local store and cleaning.
📍 Close to amazing scenery: rainforest, mountains, and glaciers.

4 GRAMMAR *be going to*

a ▶ **12.04** Complete the sentences from the conversations. Listen and check your answers.
1 I'm _____ to email and ask about it.
2 I'm _____ to quit this job.

b Look at the sentences in 4a. Underline the correct words to complete the rule.

> We use *be* + *going to* + infinitive when we want to describe *a future plan / a present action*.

c ▶ **12.05** Complete the sentences with the correct forms of *be going to* and the verbs in parentheses. Listen and check your answers.
+ I _____ (find out) more about it.
– I _____ (not go) to college next year.
? What _____ (do)?

d ▶ **12.05** **Pronunciation** Listen to the sentences in 4c again. How is *going to* often pronounced? Which is stressed, *going* or the main verb?

e ≫ Now go to Grammar Focus 12A on p. 160.

f ▶ **12.07** Complete the conversation with *be going to* and the verbs in parentheses. Listen and check your answers.

A I ¹_____ (spend) six months traveling and working next year.
B Great. Where are you ²_____ (go)?
A I ³_____ (travel) around South Africa.
B What jobs ⁴_____ (do)?
A Cleaning, cooking, working in restaurants – things like that. I ⁵_____ (not do) anything too difficult.
B And what about after your trip?
A I ⁶_____ (look) for a job at home.

5 SPEAKING

a 💬🗣 Talk about which of the three working vacations you would like to do.

b ≫ **Communication 12A** Student A go to p. 135. Student B go to p. 137.

1 READING

a 💬 Ask and answer the questions.

Would you like to live in a different country? Why / Why not? If yes, which country would you choose?

b Read the article and match the people with pictures a–d.

c Read the sentences. Who do you think wrote each one: Troy (*T*), Oliver and Kirsten (*OK*), or Avery (*A*)?

1 Saw some beautiful fish yesterday. Fantastic!
2 We have a job taking photos for a local newspaper.
3 I think they liked the music I played last night.
4 I'm going to work on the island of Koh Tao – the sea is so clear there.
5 We're going to find a local school for our daughter next week.

d 💬 Would you like to go traveling and never stop? Why / Why not?

Why not go **traveling** ... *and* **never** *stop?*

In 2010, Troy sold everything, packed a small bag, and left his home in Canada to travel abroad. He was 30. Ten years and 15 countries later, he's still traveling, and he says he's never going to go back home. Last year he arrived in Portugal. To earn money, Troy works as an English teacher. He's also a DJ in some local nightclubs.

TROY SAYS: *You can use English in most places, but you should try to learn the local language, too.*

Like many students, Avery graduated from college in her hometown of Portland, Oregon, and decided to take a long vacation. She stayed in cheap hotels and with friends in different countries. Five years later, she is still enjoying that vacation. When she was in Australia, she learned how to dive. She loved it, and she decided to take a class and learn to teach other people how to dive. Now she works all over the world teaching tourists to dive.

AVERY SAYS: *It's a big, wide world out there. I don't want to spend my life in just one place.*

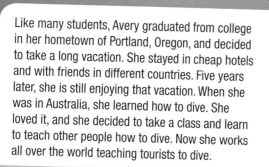

122

2 VOCABULARY Travel collocations

a Match pairs of verbs 1–6 with a word or phrase in the box. Use the texts in 1b to help you.

| a hotel   a bag   home   abroad   plans   a vacation |

1 make / change _____
2 travel / live _____
3 stay / go back _____
4 plan / take _____
5 book / stay in _____
6 pack / unpack _____

b ▶12.08 Six people talk about traveling and vacations. Complete the sentences with verbs in 2a. Listen and check your answers.

1 I always _____ my vacations carefully. I read about the place before I go there.
2 I don't want to _____ abroad. It's better to go on vacation in my own country.
3 I never _____ a hotel. I want to see my room before I decide to stay there.
4 I usually _____ my bags about an hour before I go on vacation. I hate doing it!
5 After a week away, I'm always happy to _____ home and see my family again.
6 When I'm on vacation, I never _____ plans. I just see what happens when I get there.

c 💬 Which speakers in 2b do you agree with? Why / Why not?

3 GRAMMAR should / shouldn't

a Look at the sentences. <u>Underline</u> the correct words. Then check in the texts.

1 You *should / shouldn't* try to learn the local language, too.
2 You *should / shouldn't* forget your family back home.
3 You *should / shouldn't* live like the local people.

Oliver and Kirsten Foster left the UK in 2013. In three years, they traveled to Mexico, Peru, the U.S., Thailand, China, Dubai, and Germany before arriving at their latest home in Egypt in 2016. They're both photographers, so they can work anywhere in the world. They now have a three-year-old daughter, Liona, so they have to make plans more carefully. But they don't want to change their lives. Next year they are going to live in Ecuador and then South Africa.

OLIVER SAYS: I love meeting new people, but you shouldn't forget your family back home. I call my mom every week.

KIRSTEN SAYS: You should live like the local people and try to make friends with people from the country.

b Choose the correct answer to complete the rules.

You should means ... .
a you have to do it   b it's a good idea
After *should* and *shouldn't* we use ... .
a infinitive   b the base form

c ▶12.09 **Pronunciation** Listen to sentences 2 and 3 in 3a.

1 Is there an /l/ sound in *should* and *shouldn't*?
2 Does *should* rhyme with *good* or *cold*?

d ≫ Now go to Grammar Focus 12B on p. 160.

e Read the advice about living abroad. Change the verbs in blue by adding *should* or *shouldn't*.

WOULD YOU LIKE TO LIVE ABROAD?
TAKE OUR ADVICE!

1 Don't stay at home all the time.
Go out and meet people.
You shouldn't stay at home all the time. You should …
2 Try to visit a new place every weekend.
Don't wait until the last few weeks of your stay.
3 Read about the country before you go there.
4 Don't get mad when things go wrong.
5 Remember that things work differently in other countries.

4 LISTENING AND SPEAKING

a What do you think these people mean?

| I'm a very active person. | I'm not really a city person. | I'm a beach person. |

💬 What about you and other students? Are you the same?

b 💬 Quickly read the information again about Troy and Avery. Which things below do you think Troy likes and which do you think Avery likes? Why? Write *T* (Troy) or *A* (Avery).

☐ the ocean   ☐ noise   ☐ big cities
☐ cafés   ☐ beaches   ☐ dancing
☐ sports   ☐ music
☐ shopping   ☐ the country

c ▶12.11 Listen to Troy and Avery. Check your answers in 4b.

d 💬 Troy and Avery are going to visit your country. Talk about where they should and shouldn't go, what they should do, and why.

You should go downtown. There are a lot of good cafés.

You shouldn't go to the National Museum. It's very boring!

e 💬 Work with a student you don't know very well. Find out what they like and don't like doing on vacation.

f 💬 Give your partner some advice about what to do and what not to do in a city you know.

12C EVERYDAY ENGLISH
Is breakfast included?

Julia and Diego Torres

1 LISTENING

a 💬 Ask and answer the questions.

1 When you go on vacation, where do you usually stay? Choose one or more places.
- hotel
- hostel
- camping in a tent
- apartment/house
- with friends
- another place

2 Why do you like staying in this/these place(s)?

b ▶️ 12.12 Listen to Part 1 and answer the questions.

1 Who won a contest?
2 Can Diego and Julia use the prize in June?

c ▶️ 12.12 Listen to Part 1 again. Complete the email. Put a word or number in each blank.

Dear [1]_____,
Congratulations! You have won a weekend for [2]_____ people in the city of [3]_____. All your travel and hotel expenses are included in the prize.

You must travel on [4]_____, May [5]_____. Enjoy!

2 CONVERSATION SKILLS Showing surprise

a Look at the conversation. <u>Underline</u> the two ways that Diego shows surprise.

JULIA	I won a contest!
DIEGO	You did? Julia, that's great! What's the prize?
JULIA	A weekend for two in Las Vegas …
DIEGO	Really? That's amazing!

b Which question in 2a can you use to reply to any news?

c ▶️ 12.13 Match 1–4 with a–d. Listen and check your answers.

1 I'm getting married.
2 I really like grammar.
3 I went to New York for the weekend.
4 I've eaten an insect.

a You do?
b You have?
c You are?
d You did?

d ▶️ 12.13 **Pronunciation** Listen again. Does the intonation in a–d in 2c go up ↗ a little or a lot?

e Think of two surprising things. They don't have to be true! Take notes.

f 💬 In pairs, take turns telling each other your surprising things and showing surprise. Use expressions from 2a and 2c.

3 LISTENING

a ▶️ 12.14 Look at the picture. What do you think the hotel is like? Do you think Julia and Diego will like it? Listen to Part 2 and check.

b ▶️ 12.14 Listen to Part 2 again. Complete the guest information card.

WELCOME TO THE

IMPERIAL
HOTEL

Your room number is [1]_____.
Please join us for breakfast in the dining room from [2]_____ to [3]_____.
Your checkout time is [4]_____.

ENJOY YOUR STAY.

4 USEFUL LANGUAGE
Checking in at a hotel

a Below are useful expressions for hotel guests. Which two expressions did Julia use?

1 I have a reservation for a double room for two nights.
2 Is there a parking lot?
3 Is breakfast included?
4 Is there Wi-Fi in the room?
5 What time is checkout?
6 Is there a safe in the room?

b Which four questions in 4a do we use to ask about things hotels can offer?

c ▶12.15 Complete the conversation between a guest and a hotel receptionist with sentences from 4a. Listen and check your answers.

RECEPTIONIST	Hello, how can I help you?
GUEST	Hello. I ¹_____.
RECEPTIONIST	A double room? Your name, please?
GUEST	Barnes.
RECEPTIONIST	Thank you. So, that's two nights?
GUEST	Yes. Is ²_____?
RECEPTIONIST	Yes, it's from 6:30 a.m. until 9:30 a.m. in the dining room.
GUEST	Is ³_____?
RECEPTIONIST	Yes, there is. There's no password to log in.
GUEST	And what ⁴_____?
RECEPTIONIST	It's 11 o'clock on the day you leave.

5 PRONUNCIATION
Consonant clusters

a ▶12.16 Listen to these sentences. Notice how the consonant clusters in **bold** with /t/ are pronounced.

1 I have a reservation for a double room for two ni**ghts**.
2 So, tha**t's** two ni**ghts**?
3 Is breakfa**st** included?
4 I**t's** from 6:30 a.m. until 9:30 a.m.

b ▶12.17 Listen to these sentences below. Underline consonant clusters with /t/.

1 We're busy next weekend.
2 I'd like some tourist information.
3 The bathroom is on your left.
4 Can I buy two tickets, please?

c 💬 In pairs, practice conversations like the one in 4c. Use your own name and change some of the questions about things in the hotel. Take turns being the receptionist and guest.

6 LISTENING

a ▶12.18 Listen to Part 3. Complete the information on Las Vegas bus tours.

Las Vegas
BUS TOURS

Leaves from ¹_____
Price ²_____
Buy tickets at ³_____
Pay by cash or ⁴_____

b 💬 Why did Julia and Diego change hotels? What do you think the bus tour is like?

7 USEFUL LANGUAGE
Asking for tourist information

a ▶12.19 Match 1–5 with a–e to complete the questions. Listen and check your answers.

1 Can you   a for a ticket?
2 Is there a city bus tour   b two tickets, please.
3 How much is it   c help us?
4 Can we buy   d we can go on?
5 We'll take   e tickets here in the hotel lobby?

b You are on vacation and go to a tourist information office to ask about an interesting museum to visit. Answer the questions.

1 Can you use all the questions in 7a?
2 Which one(s) do you have to change?
3 Write a new question for the example(s) you need to change.

c 💬 Work in pairs. Use your answers in 7b to make a conversation at the tourist information office about visiting a museum. Take turns being the tourist and an assistant who works in the office.

8 SPEAKING

a ≫ **Communication 12C** Student A go to p. 135. Student B go to p. 137.

✓ UNIT PROGRESS TEST

→ CHECK YOUR PROGRESS

You can now do the Unit Progress Test.

12D | SKILLS FOR WRITING
You should go to Stanley Park

1 SPEAKING AND LISTENING

a How much do you plan your vacations before you leave? Choose an answer and say why.

1 I like to plan everything as much as possible so I know what I'm going to do.
2 I plan my travel and accommodations, but nothing else.
3 I only buy tickets. I figure out everything else when I arrive.

b 💬 Look at the pictures of places in Vancouver and answer the questions.

1 What do you know about Vancouver and Canada?
2 What can you see in the pictures?

c ▶ 12.20 Zach tells Tiffany about a vacation he's planned. Listen and underline the correct answers.

1 Zach booked his vacation *online* / *at a travel agency*.
2 He's going to go to Vancouver for a *weekend* / *week*.
3 He's going to stay in a *hostel* / *hotel*.
4 He's going to go at the end of *this* / *next* month.
5 *Tiffany* / *Zach* has a friend named Nicole in Vancouver.

d 💬 You want to visit Vancouver. What questions could you ask Nicole?

> What should I see in Vancouver?

2 READING

a Zach sent Nicole an email. Read Nicole's reply. What *doesn't* she talk about?

   a places to visit   b the hostel   c the weather

Re: Vancouver

Hi Zach,

¹Thanks for your email. ²I'm really happy to help you plan your vacation in Vancouver. ³I've been here for two years now, and I just love it. ⁴I'm sure you're going to have a great time here. ⁵You asked me about the three top tourist things to do in Vancouver, so here are some ideas. ⁶First, you should visit my favorite part of the downtown area: Gastown. ⁷It's a mix of historic and modern stores and restaurants – it looks like a street from more than a hundred years ago. ⁸And second, you should go to Stanley Park – an amazing green area in the middle of town with forests and beaches, and a really big aquarium. ⁹Finally, the third place you should go to is Vancouver Island – it's about 60 miles away from the city. ¹⁰Catch a ferry and stay a couple of nights. ¹¹It's really beautiful, and there's a lot of interesting history and culture you can learn about. ¹²But you can also spend time just walking or biking around the center of Vancouver. ¹³You said you were going to come at the end of next month. ¹⁴It's fall then and it's not too hot or too cold, so it's really nice doing things outdoors. ¹⁵It's a city with so much natural beauty – I'm sure you're going to love it! ¹⁶I hope these ideas help you. ¹⁷Let's meet and get a cup of coffee when you come.

Best wishes,

Nicole

b Read Nicole's email again and complete the chart.

Place to visit	Reason to visit
Gastown	historic & ¹_____ stores & ²_____
Stanley Park	forests & ³_____ & a big ⁴_____
Vancouver Island	interesting history & ⁵_____

3 WRITING SKILLS Paragraph writing

a Read Nicole's email again. Make four paragraphs.

Paragraph 1 answers Zach and talks about Vancouver in general: Sentences 1 to ___
Paragraph 2 talks about things to do: Sentences ___ to 12
Paragraph 3 talks about the weather: Sentences 13 to ___
Paragraph 4 finishes the message: Sentences ___ to ___

b Look at Paragraph 2. Underline three linking words that order the information.

c Read the email from Alice to you and answer the questions.

  1 What is she going to do?
  2 What does she want to know?

Hi

Hi there,

¹My name is Alice, and I'm going to visit your hometown soon. ²A friend told me that you can give me useful information, so I have some questions if that's OK. ³I would like to do some sightseeing. ⁴What are some interesting things to see? ⁵I'd also like to do some kind of sports activity. ⁶What are some interesting things to do? ⁷I hope you can help me!

Alice

Kind regards,

Alice

d Make three paragraphs in Alice's email in 3c.

4 WRITING

a Plan an email to Alice.

- answer both her questions
- use paragraphs for different parts of your message
- use linking words to order your ideas.

b Write your email. Use Nicole's email to help you.

c Switch emails with another student and check.

☐ Are the paragraphs clear?
☐ Are there good ideas of things to see and do?
☐ Are there linking words to order ideas?

UNIT 12
Review and extension

1 GRAMMAR

a Complete the sentences with the correct form of *be going to* and a verb from the box.

travel   move   wear   have

1 He turns 30 next week. He _____ a big party.
2 When we're older, we _____ to a cottage in the country.
3 I _____ my new suit and a tie for my interview.
4 She has two months off before she starts college, so she _____ around Europe with a friend.

b Write the conversation using the prompts with the correct form of *be going to*.

PAULINA [1]What / you / do after graduation?
What are you going to do after graduation?
NATALIA [2]I / go to New York.
PAULINA New York? Sounds great. [3]What / you / do there?
NATALIA Well, my brother lives there.
PAULINA Oh, right. [4]you / stay / with / him?
NATALIA Yes. He says [5]he / find / me / a job.
PAULINA Oh, really? [6]How long / you / stay?
NATALIA Just a month. But [7]I not / book my flight back. Who knows? If I find a good job, I may stay longer!

c Read the travel advice to people going to Kenya in East Africa. Complete the text with *you should* or *you shouldn't*.

It's very hot in Kenya, so [1]_____ stay in the sun for too long, and [2]_____ drink a lot of water. [3]_____ buy bottled water, and [4]_____ drink water from lakes or rivers.

Most people speak English, but [5]_____ try to learn a few words of Swahili, the local language.

2 VOCABULARY

a Underline the correct words.

1 We went to a Greek *island* / *mountain*. We just sat on the *forest* / *beach* and swam in the sea. It was very relaxing.
2 I went across the Gobi *Desert* / *Lake* on a camel.
3 I watched birds in the Brazilian *desert* / *rainforest*.
4 The Iguazu Falls are big *waterfalls* / *mountains* between Argentina and Brazil.
5 I climbed *rivers* / *mountains* in Norway, and we crossed a *glacier* / *beach*. It was very cold on the ice.

b Put the words in the correct order to make questions.

1 you / abroad / lived / ever / have?
2 you / planned / your next vacation / have?
3 in a hotel / last / stay / you / did / when?
4 always / you / your own bags / pack / do / for a vacation?
5 this weekend / you / home / are / staying?

c 💬🗨 Ask and answer the questions in 2b.

3 WORDPOWER *take*

a Match sentences 1–6 with pictures a–f. What do you think the people are talking about?

1 You can take the number 23.
2 Please take care!
3 It will only take five minutes.
4 Then you take the first left.
5 Let me take your suitcase for you.
6 Take one three times a day before meals.

b Match the sentences in 3a with the uses of *take* in a–f.

a to give street directions
b to talk about time
c to tell someone to be careful
d to talk about using transportation
e to talk about medicine
f to talk about carrying something

▶ **12.21** Listen to the conversations and check.

c Complete the sentences with *take* and a word or phrase in the box.

a taxi   the first left   hours
my medicine   my laptop   care

1 I have two essays to write. It will _____ to finish my homework.
2 There aren't any buses. Why don't we _____?
3 Have a great vacation and _____.
4 Go straight until you come to a supermarket, then _____.
5 I'll carry the bags, but could you _____?
6 Oh, it's six o'clock. Time to _____.

d Choose two of the uses of *take* in 3b. Write a short conversation using examples of both uses.

e 💬🗨 Practice your conversations in 3d.

🔄 REVIEW YOUR PROGRESS

How well did you do in this unit? Write 3, 2, or 1 for each objective.
3 = very well   2 = well   1 = not so well

I CAN ...	
talk about vacation plans	☐
give advice	☐
talk about travel	☐
use language for travel and tourism	☐
write an email with travel advice	☐

Phonemic symbols

Vowel sounds

/ə/	/æ/	/ʊ/	/ɑ/	/ɪ/	/i/	/e/	/ʌ/	/ɜ/	/u/	/ɔ/
breakf**a**st	m**a**n	p**u**t	g**o**t	ch**i**p	happ**y**	m**e**n	**u**p	sh**ir**t	wh**o**	w**a**lk

Diphthongs (two vowel sounds)

/eə/	/ɪə/	/ɔɪ/	/aɪ/	/eɪ/	/oʊ/	/aʊ/
h**air**	n**ear**	b**oy**	n**i**ne	**ei**ght	wind**ow**	n**ow**

Consonants

/p/	/b/	/f/	/v/	/t/	/d/	/k/	/g/
picnic	**b**ook	**f**ace	**v**ery	**t**ime	**d**og	**c**old	**g**o
/θ/	/ð/	/tʃ/	/dʒ/	/s/	/z/	/ʃ/	/ʒ/
think	**th**e	**ch**air	**j**ob	**s**ea	**z**oo	**sh**oe	televi**si**on
/m/	/n/	/s/	/h/	/l/	/r/	/w/	/j/
me	**n**ow	si**ng**	**h**ot	**l**ate	**r**ed	**w**ent	**y**es

Irregular verbs

Infinitive	Simple past		Infinitive	Simple past
be	was		meet	met
begin	began		pay	paid
buy	bought		put	put
catch	caught		read	read
choose	chose		ride	rode
come	came		run	ran
do	did		say	said
drink	drank		see	saw
drive	drove		sell	sold
eat	ate		send	sent
feel	felt		sing	sang
find	found		sit	sat
fly	flew		sleep	slept
forget	forgot		speak	spoke
get	got		swim	swam
give	gave		take	took
go	went		teach	taught
grow up	grew up		tell	told
have	had		think	thought
hear	heard		understand	understood
know	knew		wake up	woke up
leave	left		wear	wore
lose	lost		write	wrote

COMMUNICATION PLUS

9A STUDENT A

a Look at your picture for two minutes. What are the people doing? Make notes.

b Student B has a similar picture. Ask and answer questions to find five differences.

> Is Ken drinking coffee in your picture?

> Yes, he is. / No, he's not. He's …

11C STUDENT A

a **Conversation 1.** Read your first card. Think about what you want to say. Then listen to Student B and reply about the concert.

1 You went with Student B to a concert last night. You thought the band was really good. You like their music, and you thought the singer was good.

b **Conversation 2.** Now look at your second card. Think about what you want to say. Then start a conversation about your meal with Student B.

2 You went with Student B to Al Dente, an Italian restaurant, last weekend. You didn't like it. You had fish, but it wasn't good, and it was expensive. You thought the servers were unfriendly.

8C STUDENT B

a **Conversation 1.** Read your first card. Think about what you want to say. Then listen to Student A and reply.

1 You're not feeling very well. You're very tired and your back hurts. You don't have a fever. When Student A asks you, tell him/her what's the matter.

b **Conversation 2.** Now look at your second card. Think about what you want to say. Then start the conversation with Student A.

2 Student A doesn't look good. Ask him/her what's the matter. When he/she tells you, show sympathy using expressions like *Oh no!* or *That's too bad.*
Then ask if he/she feels hungry. Tell him/her what to do, e.g., *See a doctor. Take an aspirin. Have some soup.*

10A STUDENT A

a Ask Student B about his/her smartphone. You can use these questions:

How long is your smartphone?
How wide is your smartphone?
How big is the screen?
How much does it weigh?

b Look at the picture of your new smartphone. Compare your phone with Student B's.

c ⫸ Now go back to p. 101.

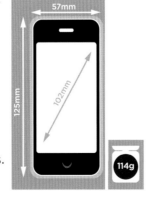

> My phone is bigger than yours.

134

12A STUDENT A

a You're going to go on a working vacation. Look at your plans.

 < Notes 28 Nov 15:46

WHERE: Australia and Pacific islands

WHY: see beautiful beaches, visit the desert in Australia

HOW LONG: three months

POSSIBLE JOBS: hotels and restaurants

BEFORE TRIP: look online for jobs

AFTER TRIP: go to college

b Student B is planning his/her own working vacation. Write questions you can ask him/her about the trip. Use 4f on page 121 to help you.

c Have a conversation with Student B about his/her vacation.

d Listen to Student B's questions about your vacation and reply.

e ⟫ Now go back to p. 121.

12C STUDENT A

a **Conversation 1.** Read your first card. Think about what you want to say. Then start the conversation with Student B.

> ① You're a guest at a hotel. You have a reservation for a double room for two nights. Check with the receptionist about:
> - the breakfast time   • Wi-Fi in the room
>
> Ask about this tourist information:
> - interesting local markets near the hotel

b **Conversation 2.** Now look at your second card. Then listen to Student B and reply.

> ② You're a hotel receptionist. Check the guest's name and let him/her know they have a reservation. Here is other information you need:
> - checkout: 10:30 a.m.
> - safe in the room
> - free box of chocolates in the room
>
> Some important tourist information about Central Park:
> - on the same street as the hotel
> - only half a kilometer away from the hotel
> - large and beautiful park

10C STUDENT B

a Conversation 1. Read your first card. Think about what you want to say. Then listen to Student A and reply.

> Student A bought a new phone, but he/she can't receive any text messages on it. When he/she asks for help, explain how it works. Here are the instructions:
> - Touch the box that says *Messages*.
> - Wait for a blue screen.
> - Touch the box that says *Receive*. It can receive messages now.

b Conversation 2. Now look at your second card. Think about what you want to say. Then start the conversation with Student A.

> You bought a new mouse for your computer, but it isn't working. Ask Student A for help. Check the instructions he/she gives you.

11C STUDENT B

a Conversation 1. Read your first card. Think about what you want to say. Start a conversation about the concert with Student A.

> You went with Student A to a concert last night. You didn't like the band very much. You thought they played badly and the music was boring.

b Conversation 2. Now look at your second card. Think about what you want to say. Then listen to Student A and reply about your meal.

> You went with Student A to Al Dente, an Italian restaurant, last weekend. You liked it. You had a very good pizza, and you thought the food was delicious and not too expensive.

9A STUDENT B

a Look at your picture for two minutes. What are the people doing? Make notes.

b Student A has a similar picture. Ask and answer questions to find five differences.

> Is Ken eating a sandwich in your picture?

> Yes, he is. / No, he's not. He's …

10A STUDENT B

a Ask Student A about his/her smartphone. You can use these questions:

How long is your smartphone?
How wide is your smartphone?
How big is the screen?
How much does it weigh?

b Look at the picture of your new smartphone. Compare your phone with Student A's.

c ⟫ Now go back to p. 101.

My screen is wider than yours.

12A STUDENT B

a You're going to go on a working vacation. Look at your plans.

⟨ Notes   18 Dec 15:46

WHERE: Central America
WHY: see rainforests, old Maya and Aztec buildings
HOW LONG: four months
POSSIBLE JOBS: taking care of children, tour guide
BEFORE TRIP: send email to friends
AFTER TRIP: find a new job

b Student A is planning his/her own working vacation. Write questions you can ask him/her about the trip. Use 4f on page 121 to help you.

c Listen to Student A's questions about your vacation and reply.

d Have a conversation with Student A about his/her vacation.

e ⟫ Now go back to p. 121.

12C STUDENT B

a **Conversation 1.** Read your first card. Then listen to Student A and reply.

1   You're a hotel receptionist. Check the guest's name and let him/her know they have a reservation. Here is other information you need:
   • breakfast 7–9:30 a.m.   • free Wi-Fi in the room
   • free dinner at the hotel tomorrow night

   Some important tourist information about a local market:
   • in a parking lot across from the hotel
   • biggest market in town
   • clothes, paintings, old furniture

b **Conversation 2.** Now look at your second card. Think about what you want to say. Then start the conversation with Student A.

2   You're a guest at a hotel. You have a reservation for a single room for three nights. Check with the receptionist about:
   • checkout time   • safe in the room

   Ask about this tourist information:
   • nice parks and gardens to visit near the hotel

GRAMMAR FOCUS

7A Simple past: negative and questions

 07.06

		+		–
I / he / she / it / you / we / they	I	**enjoyed** the trip.	He **didn't**	**enjoy** the trip.
	I	**took** the train.	He **didn't**	**take** the train.

	Yes/No questions		Short answers	
I / he / she / it / you / we / they	**Did** they	**enjoy** the trip?	Yes,	they **did**.
	Did they	**take** the train?	No,	they **didn't**.

	Wh- questions		
I / he / she / it / you / we / they	Where	**did** you	**go**?

◯ Tip
Remember, don't change the main verb in questions and negatives:
I didn't **enjoy** it. (NOT I didn't enjoyed it.)
Did you **enjoy** it? (NOT Did you enjoyed it?)

7B *love / like / don't mind / hate* + verb + *-ing*

 07.12

☺☺☺	I **love** driving!
☺	I **like** driving.
☹	I **don't mind** driving.
☹	I **don't like** driving.
☹☹☹	I **hate** driving!

After *like*, *love*, *hate*, and *don't mind*, we can use a noun or a verb + *-ing*.
I love **my car**.   I love **driving**.

SPELLING: verb + *-ing*

most verbs → add *-ing*	watch → watch**ing** go → go**ing** see → see**ing**
verb ends in consonant (*g, n, t,* etc.) + *-e* → take away the *-e* then add *-ing*	drive → driv**ing** use → us**ing**
verb ends in one vowel (*a, e, i, o, u*) and one consonant (*g, n, t,* etc.) → double the consonant and add *-ing*	run → run**ning** sit → sit**ting**
never double the consonants *w, x,* or *y* → add *-ing* only	know → know**ing** play → play**ing**

I **don't mind riding** the subway. I **like being** with other people.

7A Simple past: negative and questions

a Complete the sentences with the simple past forms of the verbs in parentheses.

1 We __didn't travel__ (not travel) by plane to Denmark – we took trains.
2 I _____ (not take) an umbrella today, so I got wet.
3 Marion and Neil _____ (not want) a big wedding.
4 He _____ (not answer) the telephone because he was busy.
5 When I was a child, I _____ (not like) chocolate.
6 We _____ (not see) any wild animals when we went to Egypt.
7 She _____ (not get) back home on time, so I was really worried.

b Change the affirmative simple past verbs to negative verb forms in these sentences.

1 We went by bus.
   _____ We didn't go by bus. _____
2 They traveled to Playa Blanca.
   _____
3 We had a good time.
   _____
4 The tickets cost a lot of money.
   _____
5 She visited China.
   _____
6 They stayed in hotels.
   _____
7 The people spoke English, so I understood them.
   _____

c Complete the questions and answers.

1 **A** _____Did_____ you _____go_____ (go) to Alaska?
   B Yes, I _____did_____.
2 **A** _____ you _____ (spend) a lot of money?
   B No, I _____.
3 **A** _____ he _____ (enjoy) his trip?
   B No, he _____.
4 **A** _____ they _____ (travel) by train?
   B Yes, they _____.

d Write the questions to complete the conversation.

A 1 _____ How did you travel? _____
   (how)
B We traveled by train.
A 2 _____
   (how much)
B The trip cost $600.
A 3 _____
   (how many)
B We visited five countries.
A 4 _____
   (where)
B We stayed in hotels.
A 5 _____
   (when)
B We arrived home yesterday.

e ≫ Now go back to p. 71.

7B love / like / don't mind / hate + verb + -ing

a Write the -ing form of the verbs.

1 wait _____waiting_____
2 drive _____
3 walk _____
4 get _____
5 fly _____
6 relax _____
7 be _____
8 have _____
9 speak _____
10 sit _____
11 stand _____
12 stay _____
13 run _____
14 try _____
15 use _____
16 agree _____

b Write sentences about Jamie and Lisa.

	eat in restaurants	cook	get pizza	try new food
Jamie	☹	😐	😐	☺☺☺
Lisa	☺	☹☹☹	☹	☺☺☺

1 Jamie _____doesn't like eating in restaurants._____
   He _____
   _____
   _____
2 Lisa _____
   She _____
   _____
   _____

c Circle the correct symbols and write sentences that are true for you.

1 wait for buses
   ☺☺☺ / ☺ / ☺ / ☹ / ☹☹☹
   _____I don't mind waiting for buses._____
2 sit in traffic
   ☺☺☺ / ☺ / 😐 / ☹ / ☹☹☹
   _____
3 play computer games
   ☺☺☺ / ☺ / 😐 / ☹ / ☹☹☹
   _____
4 fly in airplanes
   ☺☺☺ / ☺ / 😐 / ☹ / ☹☹☹
   _____
5 cook dinner
   ☺☺☺ / ☺ / 😐 / ☹ / ☹☹☹
   _____

d ≫ Now go back to p. 73.

8A *can / can't, could / couldn't* for ability

We use *can/can't* to talk about present abilities:
*I **can** read English, but I **can't** speak it.*
We use *could/couldn't* to talk about past abilities:
*When I was young, I **could** dance, but I **couldn't** sing.*

▶ 08.02

		+		–	
I / he / she / it / you / we / they	**Present**	*I **can***	*run fast.*	*They **can't***	*run fast.*
	Past	*He **could***	*run fast.*	*We **couldn't***	*run fast.*

		Yes/No questions		Short answers	
I / he / she / it / you / we / they	**Present**	***Can** you*	*run fast?*	*Yes,* / *No,*	*I **can**.* / *I **can't**.*
	Past	***Could** you*	*run fast?*	*Yes,* / *No,*	*I **could**.* / *I **couldn't**.*

> ◯ **Tip**
> There is no *-s* on *can* for *he / she / it*:
> *He **can** swim.*
> (NOT *He cans swim.*)

> ◯ **Tip**
> The full form of *can't* is *cannot*.

How fast can you run?

Well, when I was a boy, I could run pretty fast, but ...

8B *have to / don't have to*

We use *have to* + infinitive to talk about things we need to do:
*I **have to drink** a lot of water when I go running.*
*She **has to get up** at six every day.*
We can use *have to* to talk about rules:
*We **have to take off** our shoes before we go inside.*
*We **have to get to** school by nine.*
Don't have to means we don't need to do something.
*I **don't have to pay** for my lunch at work.* (My lunch is free.)
*Our teacher **doesn't have to wear** a suit.* (There is no rule.)

> ◯ **Tip**
> Sometimes, *you* means *everybody* or *people* generally.
> **A** *Do **you** have to be in shape to run a marathon?*
> (= *Do **people** have to be in shape ... ?*)
> **B** *Yes, **you** do.* (NOT *Yes, I do.*)

▶ 08.07

		+		–	
I / you / we / they	*I*	**have to** *work* hard.	*I **don't***	**have to** *work* hard.	
he / she / it	*She*	**has to work** *hard.*	*He **doesn't***	**have to** *work* hard.	

		Yes/No questions		Short answers	
I / you / we / they	***Do** you*	**have to** *work* hard?	*Yes,* / *No,*	*I **do**.* / *I **don't**.*	
he / she / it	***Does** he*	**have to** *work* hard?	*Yes,* / *No,*	*he **does**.* / *he **doesn't**.*	

If you're tired, you don't **have to** run anymore. You can walk.

8A *can / can't, could / couldn't* for ability

a Complete the sentences with *can/can't, could/couldn't*.

1　I ____can____ play the guitar. I want to learn the drums next.

2　I _____ drive last year, but I passed my test six weeks ago!

3　She _____ cook really well. Her food is always great.

4　He isn't on the soccer team, because he _____ run very fast.

5　When I was in school, I _____ do math. But now I'm much better.

6　My husband _____ speak French, Spanish, and Portuguese. It's useful when we travel!

7　I _____ climb trees when I was a child, but I'm too old now.

b Write sentences about what Rob *could/couldn't* do in the past and what he *can/can't* do now.

When he was a boy	Now
swim 1,000 meters ✗	swim 1,000 meters ✓
cook a meal ✗	cook a meal ✓
ride a bike ✓	ride a bike ✗
run 25 km ✗	run 25 km ✓
speak Spanish ✗	speak Spanish ✓

1　*Rob couldn't swim 1,000 meters when he was a boy. He can swim 1,000 meters now.*

2　_____

3　_____

4　_____

5　_____

c Find and correct a mistake in each sentence.

1　I don't can play the guitar. *I can't play the guitar.*

2　She cans speak four languages. _____

3　How fast you can swim? _____

4　I could ran very fast when I was a child. _____

5　I didn't could understand what he said. _____

6　**A** Does he can cook? **B** Yes, he can. _____

7　**A** Could he walk before his accident? **B** Yes, he did. _____

d ⟫ Now go back to p. 80.

8B *have to / don't have to*

a Match questions 1–8 with answers a–h.

1　☐d　Do we have to take our shoes off?
2　☐　How much do you have to pay for a ticket?
3　☐　Do you have to be a member to use the swimming pool?
4　☐　Does she have to walk home?
5　☐　Do you have to walk the dog every day?
6　☐　Do you have to help in the kitchen?
7　☐　I want to stay at home. Why do I have to go for a walk?
8　☐　What time do you have to leave for work?

a　Because you have to stay in shape.
b　No, I don't. My parents cook and clean for me.
c　Yes, I do. Every day.
d　No, you don't. You can keep them on.
e　At eight o'clock.
f　Nothing. It's free.
g　No, you don't. It's open to everybody.
h　No, she doesn't. She has enough money for a taxi.

b Complete the sentences with the correct form of *have to* or a short answer.

1　In a kitchen, ____you have to work____ (you / work) very carefully.

2　**A** _____ (you / buy) any new clothes for your new job?
　B Yes, _____.

3　_____ (I / not / pay) rent right now, because I'm living with my parents.

4　I usually wear jeans and a T-shirt, but at work _____ (I / wear) a suit.

5　**A** What _____ (we / do) before we start the game?
　B I don't know. Read the instructions.

6　**A** Do _____ (I / give) them a present?
　B No, _____. But it's a nice idea.

7　My son would like to see this movie. How old _____ (he / be)?

8　To get in shape, I think _____ (you / walk) for at least half an hour a day.

c Put a check (✓) or an *X* (✗) next to each activity and write sentences that are true for you.

1　I / study for three hours every evening ✓
　I have to study for three hours every evening.

2　I / cook dinner every night ✗
　I don't have to cook dinner every night.

3　I / do a lot of homework
　_____

4　My teacher / help me with grammar
　_____

5　My best friend / sometimes / wait for me
　_____

6　My father / go to work at eight o'clock
　_____

d ⟫ Now go back to p. 81.

9A Present continuous

We use the present continuous to describe an activity now or at the moment of speaking. The activity started in the past and will finish in the future.

▶ 09.08

	+		−	
I	I'm	waiting.	I'm not	waiting.
you / we / they	You're	waiting.	We're not	waiting.
he / she / it	He's	waiting.	He's not	waiting.

There are two different contractions for *is not* and *are not*.

is not → *'s not / isn't*: He**'s not** = He **isn't**

are not → *'re not / aren't*: We**'re not** = We **aren't**

Full forms: *am waiting, are waiting, is waiting; am not waiting, are not waiting, is not waiting*

	Yes/No questions		Short answers	
I	**Am** I	waiting?	Yes, No,	I **am**. I**'m not**.
you / we / they	**Are** you	waiting?	Yes, No,	you **are**. you**'re not**.
he / she / it	**Is** he	waiting?	Yes, No,	he **is**. he**'s not**.

	Wh- questions		
I	Why	**am** I	waiting?
you / we / they	Where	**are** you	waiting?
he / she / it	Who	**is** he	waiting for?

talk to you

Past   Now   Future

9B Simple present or present continuous

The simple present is about things that are normally true. We use it to describe habits, routines, facts, and feelings:
*I usually **wear** pants.*   *He **loves** cars.*

The present continuous is about now. We use it to describe what is happening now / today / this week etc.:
*Today I'm **wearing** a dress.*   *I'm **studying** hard this week.*

There are some verbs which we don't usually use in the present continuous:

like   love   hate   not mind   want   know
need   understand   remember   forget

*I **want** to go home.* (NOT *I'm wanting to go home.*)

> 💬 **Tip**
> We don't use *have* for possession in continuous sentences:
> *I **have** a new car.* (NOT *I'm having a new car.*)
> *She **has** red hair.* (NOT *She's having red hair.*)
> We can use *have* for actions in continuous sentences:
> *We're **having** dinner right now.*
> *I'm **not having** fun.*

Me the day before yesterday   Me yesterday   I usually wear trousers ... but today I'm wearing a dress!   Me tomorrow   Me the day after tomorrow

Past   Now   Future

9A Present continuous

a Write about the pictures using the present continuous.

he / drink / coffee
1 _He's drinking coffee._

I / do / a grammar exercise
4 _____

they / talk
2 _____

she / not / wear / shoes
5 _____

he / not / ride / a horse
3 _____

they / play / tennis
6 _____

b Complete the conversations using the present continuous and the verbs in parentheses. Use short answers where possible.

1 **A** Who ___are___ you ___waiting___ (wait) for?
  B I ____'m____ ___waiting___ (wait) for you.
2 **A** Why _____ she _____ (smile)?
  B I don't know. Maybe she _____ _____ (feel) happy.
3 **A** _____ you _____ (sleep)?
  B No, I _____ _____ .
4 **A** Where _____ they _____ (stand)?
  B They _____ _____ _____ (not stand). They're sitting at a table.
5 **A** _____ your brother _____ (play) soccer today?
  B No, he _____ _____ . He _____ _____ (play) basketball.

c Complete the telephone conversation using the present continuous forms of the words in parentheses.

A What [1] ___are you doing___ (you / do)?
B [2] _____ (I / shop) downtown. Where are you?
A [3] _____ (We / look) for a parking space. [4] _____ (we / drive) past the museum.
B Really? [5] _____ (I / stand) outside the museum right now!
A I can't see you. What [6] _____ (you / wear)?
B [7] _____ (I / wear) a red T-shirt.
A OK, I can see you now, but [8] _____ (we / not stop). The traffic is too busy!

d ⟫ Now go back to p. 91.

9B Simple present or present continuous

a Choose the correct words to complete the sentences.

1 She _usually_ / _today_ wears black clothes.
2 She's wearing bright colors _usually_ / _today_.
3 They _never_ / _are not_ visit museums. They don't like them.
4 My parents aren't at home. They are visiting a museum _sometimes_ / _this morning_.
5 Wow! Look! Tom _dances_ / _'s dancing_! He doesn't usually dance.
6 I _enjoy_ / _'m enjoying_ the party. Thanks for inviting me!
7 I always watch soccer _on weekends_ / _at the moment_.
8 We don't go out _now_ / _often_.

b Complete the conversations with the correct form of the verbs in parentheses. Use the simple present or the present continuous.

1 **A** What ___are you doing___ (you / do)?
  B _____ (we / get) ready to go out. Would you like to come with us?
  A Not really, no. _____ (I / watch) a movie. It's really good.
2 **A** What's that noise?
  B Sorry, it's my friend Harry. _____ (he / sing).
  A Wow! He's really good.
  B Yes, _____ (he / sing) in a band every weekend. _____ (They / often / play) concerts.
3 **A** _____ (you / play) that computer game again?
  B No, _____ . _____ (I / try) to sell my guitar on the Internet.
  A Really? Why _____ (you / do) that?

c Choose the options that are true for you and write sentences.

1 wear bright colors   usually ✓   ✗   now ✓   ⓧ
  _____ _I usually wear bright colors._
  _____ _I'm not wearing bright colors now._
2 feel happy   usually ✓   ✗   now ✓   ✗
  _____
  _____
3 listen to music
  when I study   usually ✓   ✗   now ✓   ✗
  _____
  _____
4 wear a watch   usually ✓   ✗   now ✓   ✗
  _____
  _____
5 use a computer
  when I study   usually ✓   ✗   now ✓   ✗
  _____
  _____
6 study in my
  bedroom   usually ✓   ✗   now ✓   ✗
  _____
  _____

d ⟫ Now go back to p. 93.

10A Comparative adjectives

▶ 10.02

We use a comparative adjective + *than* to compare two or more things, people, etc.

*My new smartphone is **bigger than** my old one.*   *My phone is **more expensive than** my sister's.*
*My tablet is **heavier than** my phone.*   *Your laptop is **better than** mine.*

One syllable	End in -*y*	Two or more syllables
adjective + -*er*	adjective – -*y* + -*ier*	*more* + adjective
old → old**er**	heavy → heav**ier**	useful → **more** useful
cheap → cheap**er**	easy → eas**ier**	expensive → **more** expensive
light → light**er**	pretty → prett**ier**	difficult → **more** difficult

> 🔍 **Tip**
>
> *good* and *bad* are irregular:
> *good* → *better*   *bad* → *worse*

SPELLING: adjective + -*er*

most adjectives → add -*er*	short → short**er**
	clean → clean**er**
adjective ends in -*e* → add -*r*	larg**e** → larger
	nic**e** → nicer
adjective ends in consonant + -*y* → change -*y* to -*i* then add -*er*	dry → dr**ier**
	easy → eas**ier**
adjective ends in one vowel (*a, e, i, o, u*) and one consonant (*g, n, t*, etc.) → double the consonant and add -*er*	hot → hot**ter**
	thin → thin**ner**

Life is **easier** with new technology.

10B Superlative adjectives

We use the superlative form of adjectives to talk about extremes.
We usually use *the* before superlatives.

▶ 10.06

***The most useful** language is English.*
***The easiest** language is Spanish.*
*What's **the hardest** language in the world?*
***The best** language practice is speaking.*

> 🔍 **Tip**
>
> We don't use *the* with words like *my, your*, etc.
> She's my best friend. (NOT ~~She's my the best friend~~.)

One syllable	End in -*y*	Two or more syllables
the + adjective + -*est*	*the* + adjective – -*y* + -*iest*	*the most* + adjective
old → **the** old**est**	heavy → **the** heav**iest**	useful → **the most** useful
cheap → **the** cheap**est**	easy → **the** eas**iest**	expensive → **the most** expensive
light → **the** light**est**	pretty → **the** prett**iest**	difficult → **the most** difficult

> 🔍 **Tip**
>
> *good* and *bad* are irregular:
> *good* → *the best*   *bad* → *the worst*

SPELLING: adjective + -*est*

most adjectives → add -*est*	short → short**est**
	clean → clean**est**
adjective ends in -*e* → add -*st*	larg**e** → largest
	nic**e** → nicest
adjective ends in consonant + -*y* → change -*y* to -*i* then add -*est*	dry → dr**iest**
	easy → eas**iest**
adjective ends in one vowel (*a, e, i, o, u*) and one consonant (*g, n, t*, etc.) → double the consonant and add -*est*	hot → hot**test**
	thin → thin**nest**

10A Comparative adjectives

a Write the comparative form of the adjectives.

1 angry _____angrier_____
2 bad _____
3 clean _____
4 cold _____
5 comfortable _____
6 crowded _____
7 fast _____
8 fat _____
9 good _____
10 interesting _____
11 modern _____
12 noisy _____
13 old _____
14 popular _____
15 sad _____
16 strange _____
17 strong _____
18 thin _____
19 wet _____
20 wide _____

b Write sentences using the simple present of *be* and comparative adjectives.

1 my new phone / cheap / my old phone
    _____My new phone is cheaper than my old phone._____
2 the movie / interesting / the book
    _____
3 her children / noisy / my children
    _____
4 she / a good cook / my dad
    _____
5 Dubai / modern / Dublin
    _____
6 this hotel / comfortable / the last hotel
    _____
7 my friends / funny / me
    _____

c Correct one mistake in each sentence.

1 She quicker than me. She always finishes first.
    _____
2 The book is good than the movie.
    _____
3 My grades are always worser than yours.
    _____
4 This dress is prettyer than that one.
    _____
5 Seattle's weather is weter than the weather in Arizona. _____
6 Their family is more big than mine.
    _____
7 My new teacher is most interesting than my old teacher. _____
8 Is your Internet faster mine? _____

d ≫ Now go back to p. 101.

10B Superlative adjectives

a Write the superlative form of the adjectives.

1 clean _____the cleanest_____
2 short _____
3 funny _____
4 dry _____
5 pretty _____
6 bad _____
7 friendly _____
8 good _____
9 big _____
10 nice _____
11 safe _____
12 exciting _____
13 tiring _____
14 hot _____

English is not **the most beautiful** language in the world.
Some people say it's not **the easiest**. But when you're lost,
it's probably **the most useful**.

b Complete the sentences using the superlative form of the adjectives in parentheses.

1 One of _____the longest_____ (long) words in English is *floccinaucinihilipilification*. But I don't know what it means!
2 _____ (short) words in English are *a* and *I*.
3 In spoken English, one of _____ (popular) words is *I* – because we think we're _____ (interesting) topic in the world!
4 _____ (useful) noun in English is *time*. We use it all the time!
5 _____ (fast) way to learn a language is to go and live in a different country.
6 Some people think _____ (important) thing for language learners is speaking.
7 I think _____ (good) way to improve your English is to learn a lot of words – I try to learn ten new words every day.
8 When you're reading in English, _____ (bad) thing you can do is check all the words in a dictionary. It takes too long and it's not much fun!

c ≫ Now go back to p. 102.

11A Present perfect

see the movie

my life

Born   Now

We use the present perfect to talk about past actions in a time period which starts in the past and continues now, for example: today, this week, this year, your lifetime.
I've seen that movie four times (*in my life*).
I haven't had any coffee *today*.
Have you *been* to the gym *this week*?

We make the present perfect from the verb *have* + the past participle of the main verb.

For regular verbs, the past participle is the same as the past form:
I *walked* to work yesterday.
I've walked to work three times this week.

For irregular verbs, the past participle is usually different. You have to learn the different forms. (See page 129 for a list of irregular verbs.)
I *drove* to work yesterday.
I've driven to work three times this week.

▶ 11.06

	+	
I / you / we / they	*I've*	*seen* the movie 400 times.
he / she / it	*He's*	*seen* the movie 400 times.

	–	
I / you / we / they	They *haven't*	*seen* the movie.
he / she / it	She *hasn't*	*seen* the movie.

We often use the present perfect to talk about experiences:
I've seen the movie once. (in my lifetime)
She*'s met* him three times. (in her lifetime)
When we ask a question about experiences, we often use the word *ever*.
Have you *ever read* this book? = Have you read this book in your lifetime?
We use *never* with the present perfect to say there is no experience.
I've never read her book. = I haven't read her book in my lifetime.

	Yes/No questions		Short answers	
I / you / we / they	*Have* you	*seen* the movie?	Yes, No,	I *have*. I *haven't*.
he / she / it	*Has* he	*seen* the movie?	Yes, No,	he *has*. he *hasn't*.

11B Present perfect or simple past

We use the present perfect to talk about the past experiences in our life, but we <u>don't</u> say when exactly.
I've been to Buenos Aires. (We don't know when.)

We use the simple past to say when something happened (e.g., *last year, yesterday, in 2012*).
I *went* to a concert *last week*. (NOT I've ~~been to the concert last week.~~)

We often start a conversation by asking about or describing an event using the present perfect, and then change to the simple past to ask about or describe the details of the event.

▶ 11.13

A *Have* you *ever been* to Argentina?   } Focus: my/your life
B Yes, I *have*. *I've been* there <u>three</u> *times*.   } Tense: present perfect

A I've been there, too. I *went* there *last year*.   } Focus: a visit last year
B Really? Which cities *did* you *visit*?   } Tense: simple past

go to Argentina

Last year   Now

I've been to Buenos Aires.

11A Present perfect

a Write the irregular past participles. Use the list on page 129 to help you.

1 see _____seen_____   6 do _____
2 write _____   7 drive _____
3 swim _____   8 ride _____
4 have _____   9 run _____
5 bring _____   10 be _____

b Complete the sentences with the present perfect forms of the verbs in parentheses.

1 I have _____read_____ (read) this book twice.
2 We _____ (visit) this museum three times this year.
3 He _____ (not borrow) my car today.
4 We _____ (never eat) at that restaurant.
5 I _____ (walk) down this street many times.
6 She _____ (play) for Peru in three Olympic Games.
7 They _____ (not do) the housework this week.
8 This country _____ (have) five big storms this winter.

c Complete the conversations with present perfect verb forms of the words in parentheses.

1
A _____Have you ever seen_____ (you / ever / see) *Star Wars*?
B Yes, _____ (I / see) it many times. It's my favorite movie.
A Really? _____ (I / never / see) it.

2
A _____ (you / ever / meet) a famous person?
B Yes, _____ (I / meet) Bill Gates.
A Wow! _____ (he / visit) Cambridge?
B Yes, _____ (he / be) here many times.

d ⟫ Now go back to p. 111.

I**'ve watched** my favorite movie 400 times.

11B Present perfect or simple past

a Underline the correct words.

1 *Have you been* / *Did you go* out last night?
2 *I've never seen* / *I never saw* an opera.
3 *We went* / *We've been* to a rock concert on Saturday.
4 *Have you ever danced* / *Did you ever dance* the tango?
5 She's a fantastic actress, but *she never won* / *she's never won* an Oscar.
6 *We've visited* / *We visited* the theater when we were in Buenos Aires last year.
7 I *didn't eat* / *'ve never eaten* sheep's milk cheese in my life.
8 *Did he win* / *Has he won* the 100m at the Olympic Games?

b Match questions 1–8 with short answers a–h.

1 [g] Did she go out?
2 [ ] Have you ever been to Chile?
3 [ ] Was it a good concert?
4 [ ] Has she been in any bad movies?
5 [ ] Were you tired when you got home?
6 [ ] Did they help you?
7 [ ] Have they ever visited Tokyo?
8 [ ] Did you have a good time?

a Yes, we were.
b Yes, we did.
c No, I haven't.
d No, they didn't.
e Yes, it was.
f No, they haven't.
g No, she didn't.
h Yes, she has.

c Complete the conversation using the correct present perfect or simple past form of the verbs in parentheses.

A ¹ _Have you ever been_ (you / ever / go) to a jazz club?
B Yes, I ² _____.
³ _____ (I / go) to a few. My favorite is *Jazz Cellar*.
⁴ _____ (I / go) there hundreds of times.
A Yes, I think ⁵ _____ (I / go) there, too. ⁶ _____ (I / go) there last year.
B ⁷ _____ (you / like) it?
A Yes, I ⁸ _____.
⁹ _____ (it / be) great. There ¹⁰ _____ (be) a wonderful singer – her name ¹¹ _____ (be) Erica something.
B Erica Sousa. ¹² _____ (I / see) her a few times. She's amazing. In fact, ¹³ _____ (she / play) a concert there last week.
A ¹⁴ _____ (you / go) to that concert?
B No, I ¹⁵ _____.
¹⁶ _____ (I / want) to go, but I had a meeting at work, and ¹⁷ _____ (I / finish) late.

d ⟫ Now go back to p. 113.

12A be going to

We use *going to* when we have a plan for the future:

▶ 12.06

		+			–	
I	I'm	**going to travel** the world next year.		I'm not	**going to work** in an office.
you / we / they	They**'re**	**going to travel** the world next year.		You**'re not**	**going to work** in an office.
he / she / it	She**'s**	**going to travel** the world next year.		He**'s not**	**going to work** in an office.

There are two different contractions for *is not* and *are not*.
is not → *'s not / isn't*: He**'s not** = He **isn't**
are not → *'re not / aren't*: You**'re not** = You **aren't**

		Yes/No questions		Short answers	
I	**Am** I	**going to travel** next year?	Yes, No,	I **am**. I**'m not**.
you / we / they	**Are** you	**going to travel** next year?	Yes, No,	you **are**. you**'re not**
he / she / it	**Is** he	**going to travel** next year?	Yes, No,	he **is**. he**'s not**.

		Wh- questions		
I	Who	**am** I	**going to travel** with?
you / we / they	Where	**are** you	**going to go**?
he / she / it	What	**'s** he	**going to see**?

I'm not going to stay in this job much longer.
I'm going to travel the world.

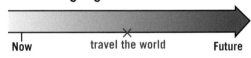

Now   travel the world   Future

12B should / shouldn't

We use *should* to give advice.
You **should** *learn the local language.* (= It's a good idea.)

▶ 12.10

	+		–	
I / he / she / it / you / we / they	I **should**	go.	They **shouldn't**	go.

	Yes/No questions		Short answers	
I / he / she / it / you / we / they	**Should** she	go?	Yes, No,	she **should**. she **shouldn't**.

	Wh- questions		
I / he / she / it / you / we / they	When	**should** we	go?

> 💡 **Tip**
> We use the infinitive without *to* after *should*.
> *You* **should take** *sunscreen with you.*
> (NOT ~~You~~ **should to take** ~~...~~)

12A be going to

a Match questions 1–8 with answers a–h.

1. [e] Where are you going to stay?
2. [ ] Are they going to visit us?
3. [ ] When are you going to clean your room?
4. [ ] Is he going to get a job?
5. [ ] Who are they going to meet?
6. [ ] Are you going to quit your job?
7. [ ] What are you going to take with you?
8. [ ] How long is he going to be away?

a Not much. Just a few clothes.
b No, he isn't. He's going to travel around the world first.
c Some of their friends.
d No, I'm not. I'm just going to take a long vacation.
e In a hotel.
f About six months.
g Tomorrow – I promise.
h No, they aren't. They don't have time.

b Complete the sentences using the correct form of *be going to* and the verb in parentheses.

1. I _____'m going to travel_____ (travel) to South America.
2. My sister _____ (get) married next year.
3. We _____ (do) a lot of sightseeing on vacation this summer.
4. They _____ (not / stay) in hotels this year.
5. My parents _____ (buy) a new house in the country.
6. I _____ (go) to the movies tonight. Do you want to come with me?
7. He _____ (not / go) to college after high school.
8. We _____ (not / visit) big cities when we go to France.
9. We _____ (stay) in small towns.

c ≫ Now go back to p. 121.

12B should / shouldn't

a Complete the sentences with the verb in parentheses and *should* or *shouldn't*.

1. **A** He feels tired all the time.
   B He ____should go____ (go) to the doctor.
2. You _____ (drink) a lot of water when you run.
3. You _____ (bring) a lot of books. We're only going for three days.
4. You _____ (drive) all night. Stop and get some sleep.
5. It's going to be cold, so you _____ (take) some warm clothes.
6. The children _____ (come) into the house – it's getting dark.
7. We _____ (pay) for the meal. The food was terrible.
8. I _____ (say) sorry to him. I broke his cup.

b Put the words in the correct order to make questions.

1. money / much / take / should / I / how ?
   ____How much money should I take?____
2. museum / we / go / a / should / to ?
   _____
3. clothes / should / what / wear / I ?
   _____
4. I / later / come / should / back ?
   _____
5. we / local / the / should / eat / food ?
   _____
6. we / should / time / arrive / what ?
   _____
7. we / where / stay / should ?
   _____
8. for / should / ask / who / we / advice ?
   _____

c Read the conversation and find six mistakes with *should*.

A I'm going to Thailand next month. Have you ever been there?
B Yes, I have.
A <u>Where should I staying?</u>
B You should look for a hotel when you arrive. You don't should book before you go.
A Really? I should go to Bangkok?
B You should to go to Bangkok for a few days, but you shouldn't stay long. You should visit an island.
A What do I should do on an island?
B Do you want to relax?
A Yes.
B You should go swimming every day. You should eat at restaurants on the beach. And you should leave your cell phone at home!
A Should I take anything with me?
B Just some money. You should not to worry about money on vacation!

d Correct the mistakes with *should* in **c**.

1. ____Where should I stay?____
2. _____
3. _____
4. _____
5. _____
6. _____

e ≫ Now go back to p. 123.

This page is intentionally left blank.

VOCABULARY FOCUS

COLLOCATIONS

7A Transportation collocations

a ▶ **07.01** Read and listen to the text. Match pictures 1–6 with phrases in **bold** a–f.

Erik works downtown, and he ᵃ**takes the train** to work every morning. He ᵇ**gets on the train** at Kings Park Station, near his home. Then he ᶜ**changes trains** at Central Station downtown, and he ᵈ**gets off** the train at Riverside Station, near his office. He usually gets to Kings Park Station at 8:00 so he can ᵉ**catch the train** at 8:05, but sometimes he's a few minutes late and he ᶠ**misses the train**. Then he has to wait for the next train.

b ▶ **07.02** Underline the correct verbs. Listen and check.

1 There were no buses, so I decided to *take / get on* a taxi.
2 It's almost 10:30. Leave now or you'll *catch / miss* the bus.
3 Excuse me. I want to go to the City Museum. Where do I *take off / get off* the bus?
4 The concert ended at 9:30, so we just *caught / changed* the last train.
5 The train was expensive, so we *take / took* a bus.
6 Quick! Let's get *on / off* the bus and find a seat! It leaves in a few minutes!

c ▶ **07.03** Pronunciation Look at these verbs and answer the question. Listen and check.

bough**t**   s**a**w   t**oo**k

Which verbs have the same sound as c**augh**t /ɔ/?

d 💬 In pairs, ask and answer the questions.

1 When was the last time … ?
   • you caught a bus or train at the last minute
   • you missed a bus or train
   • you changed trains
2 How do you get from here to your home? What kinds of transportation can you take? Where do you get on and off?

e ≫ Now go back to p. 71.

8A Sports and exercise collocations

a Match the activities in the box with pictures 1–11.

running   golf   martial arts   sailing
soccer   snowboarding   volleyball   exercises
fishing   (American) football   hockey

b Write the activities in **a** in the correct column in the chart.

go	play	do
running	golf	martial arts

c Complete the rules with *go*, *play*, or *do*. We use …

1 _____ when we talk about sports, games, and music.
2 _____ when we talk about activities that end with *-ing*.
3 _____ when we talk about other activities.

d ▶ **08.04** Pronunciation Listen to the sounds in **bold** in these words. Are they the same or different?

football   ju**do**

e ▶ **08.05** Are the sounds in **bold** in these words like *football* or *judo*? Listen and check.

1 f**u**ll   3 p**oo**l   5 f**oo**d
2 g**oo**d   4 p**u**t   6 bl**ue**

f 💬 Which activities in **a** do people do in your country? Choose a sentence which is true for each activity.

a It's very popular.
b Some people do it, but not many.
c It's very unusual.
d You can't do this in my country.

> Some people go snowboarding, but not many.

g ≫ Now go back to p. 81.

APPEARANCE AND CLOTHES

8B Appearance

a Match sentences 1–4 with four of the pictures a–h.

1 He has **short straight dark** hair.
2 She has **long straight dark** hair.
3 He has **short curly dark** hair.
4 She has **long straight blonde** hair.

b Notice the order of the adjectives in **a**. Which adjective always comes first?

c ▶ 08.09 Write sentences about the other four people's hair in **a**. Listen and check.

d Write a sentence about your hair and one about a partner's hair.

e 💬 Student A: choose a picture in **a**. Student B: ask questions to guess your partner's picture. Change roles and repeat.

> Is it a man or a woman?
>
> A man.
>
> Does he have long hair?
>
> No.
>
> Is it picture f?
>
> Yes.

f Match 1–6 with a–f.

1 She looks great in everything she wears.
2 You can see he exercises a lot.
3 Here's a photo of her at the age of five.
4 He always looks great in photos.
5 He should get more exercise.
6 I don't think she eats enough.

a He's **in good shape**.
b He's getting **out of shape**.
c She looks way too **thin**.
d She was a very **pretty** girl.
e She's a very **attractive** woman.
f He's very **good-looking**.

g ▶ 08.10 **Pronunciation** Listen to these adjectives and <u>underline</u> the stressed syllable. Listen again and repeat.

prett|y   a|ttrac|tive   good-look|ing

h 💬 Talk about famous people who are:
- thin
- attractive
- good-looking
- in shape

i ≫ Now go back to p. 83.

9B Clothes

a ▶ 09.12 Read and listen to the text. Match the words in **bold** 1–8 with pictures a–h. Listen and check.

- She looked nice. She wore a red [1]**skirt** and a white shirt, and she had a blue and yellow [2]**necklace**.
- It was a hot day, so he decided to wear a [3]**T-shirt**, [4]**shorts**, and [5]**sneakers** without socks.
- I never wear [6]**jewelry** – just a [7]**watch**, of course, and my [8]**ring**.

b ▶ 09.13 **Pronunciation** Listen to this word. Which letter don't you hear?

jewelry

c ▶ 09.14 Cross out the letters you don't hear in these words. Listen and check.

1 vegetable   3 chocolate   5 comfortable
2 interesting   4 camera

d 💬 Student A: look at Picture 1 for one minute. Student B: look at Picture 2 for one minute. Try to remember everything the people are wearing. They are all words from **a** or page 93. Cover the picture and say what you remember.

e ≫ Now go back to p. 93.

9A Money and prices

a ▶09.02 Check (✓) the correct way of saying each price: a or b. Listen and check. Listen again and repeat.

1	$25	a twenty-five dollars	b five dollars and twenty
2	$4.50	a four fifty dollars	b four dollars and fifty cents
3	$0.60	a point six dollars	b sixty cents
4	$7.40	a forty cents and seven dollars	b seven dollars and forty cents
5	$0.25	a twenty-five cents	b quarter dollars
6	$28	a eight and twenty dollars	b twenty-eight dollars
7	70¢	a seven oh cents	b seventy cents
8	$15.50	a fifteen dollars and fifty cents	b fifteen and half dollars

b 💬🎤 Take turns saying these prices.

1	$2.70	5	$4.75	9	$55.90
2	$120	6	$0.60	10	$9.99
3	$4.30	7	$10.10		
4	85¢	8	$49.95		

c ≫ Now go back to p. 90.

10B High numbers

a Match phrases 1–10 with numbers a–j.

1 a/one hundred thousand
2 one million three hundred thousand
3 one hundred and twenty
4 a/one million
5 one thousand one hundred
6 one hundred thousand two hundred
7 one hundred and thirty thousand
8 one thousand one hundred and thirty
9 five million six hundred thousand
10 a/one thousand and three

a	120	e	100,200	i	1,130
b	1,003	f	1,000,000	j	130,000
c	1,100	g	1,300,000		
d	100,000	h	5,600,000		

b ▶10.09 Look at these phrases. Add *and* to four more phrases (sometimes twice). Listen and check. Listen again and repeat.

1 340 = three hundred *and* forty
2 2,002 = two thousand two
3 45,800 = forty-five thousand eight hundred
4 381,245 = three hundred eighty-one thousand two hundred forty-five
5 2,000,670 = two million six hundred seventy
6 15,680,430 = fifteen million six hundred eighty thousand four hundred thirty

c Write down a number between:

- 600 and 699
- 3,001 and 3010
- 20,000 and 20,9991
- 1,000,000 and 1,499,999

d Ask a partner to say your numbers.

e ≫ Now go back to p. 103.

11A Irregular past participles

a ▶ **11.03** Look at these past participles. What are their infinitive forms? Listen and check.

broken	read	been	caught	written	seen	had
eaten	bought	heard	flown	forgotten	fallen	grown

b Complete the questions with past participles from **a**.

1 Have you ever _____ a fish?
2 Have you ever _____ an email in English?
3 Have you ever _____ octopus?
4 Have you ever _____ in a helicopter?
5 Have you ever _____ to Paris?
6 Have you ever _____ flowers for someone?
7 Have you ever _____ your own phone number?
8 Have you ever _____ an English newspaper?
9 Have you ever _____ an elephant?
10 Have you ever _____ African music?
11 Have you ever _____ your leg?
12 Have you ever _____ breakfast in bed?
13 Have you ever _____ down the stairs?
14 Have you ever _____ vegetables?

c ▶ **11.04** Pronunciation Listen to the sound in **bold** in h**ear**d /ɜr/.

Which of these words have the same sound as h**ear**d? Listen and check.

g**ir**l h**ear** l**ear**n n**ur**se G**er**man w**or**k y**ear**

d 💬 In pairs ask and answer the questions in **b**.

e ≫ Now go back to p. 111.

12A Geography

a Read the emails. Notice the words in **bold** and write them in the pictures.

ⓐ The _____

We have a vacation home that we go to on the weekends. It's on the **coast**, but behind us is a **jungle** with a lot of very green trees. Next to the house is a small **hill**. You can walk to the top, and the view is wonderful.

ⓓ The _____

We live outside the city in the **countryside**. There are **fields** all around the house, and in the distance there are some **woods**. I like walking there. It's so quiet – I love it.

b ▶ **12.02** Pronunciation Listen to the words in **a**. Which words have more than one syllable?

c 💬 Underline the different word in each group below. Say why.

1 lake, river, field, waterfall
2 forest, hill, woods, jungle, rainforest
3 island, mountain, coast, beach

d 💬 Think of the countryside in your country. Talk about what there is and there isn't.

> In my country, there are many hills, but there's no desert. We only have two lakes, but there are about seven or eight rivers.

e ≫ Now go back to p. 120.

Acknowledgments

The authors and publishers acknowledge the following sources of copyright material and are grateful for the permissions granted. While every effort has been made, it has not always been possible to identify the sources of all the material used, or to trace all copyright holders. If any omissions are brought to our notice, we will be happy to include the appropriate acknowledgments on reprinting and in the next update to the digital edition, as applicable.

Key:
U = Unit, CL = Classroom Language, C = Communication Plus, V = Vocabulary Focus

Text
U2: We are grateful to Gabriella Scampone for granting us permission to write the text about her.

Photographs
All the photographs are sourced from Getty Images.
Front cover photography by Franz Aberham/Photolibrary/Getty Images Plus/ Getty Images; **CL:** Dragonimages/iStock/Getty Images Plus; Skynesher/E+; Drazen_/E+; Photoalto/Dinoco Greco; Hjalmeidaistock/Getty Images Plus; Studiocasper/E+; Akepong Srichaichana/Eyeem; Alesveluscek/E+; Nattawut Lakjit/Eyeem; Blackred/E+; Daydreamsgirl/iStock/Getty Images Plus; Adha Ghazali/Eyeem; Tony Robins/Photolibrary/Getty Images Plus; **U7:** Enrique Díaz/7Cero/Moment; Brian Caissie; Andrew Lightfoot/Eyeem; Pxhidalgo/iStock/ Getty Images Plus; Historic Map Works LLC/Getty Images Plus; David Sacks/ The Image Bank/Getty Images Plus; Marioguti/iStock; Glow Images, Inc/ Getty Images Plus; Aaron Foster/Digitalvision; Steve Sparrow/Cultura; Wilf Doyle/iStock Editorial/Getty Images Plus; Image Source; Georgeclerk/iStock; Jaguarblanco/iStock Editorial/Getty Images Plus; Mordolff/E+; Neil Andrews/ Eyeem; Mikhail Spaskov/iStock/Getty Images Plus; Izusck/E+; Fuse/Corbis; Colin Anderson Productions Pty Ltd/Digitalvision; Marco Brivio/The Image Bank/Getty Images Plus; Rafael Ben-Ari/Photodisc; Plattform; Mark Meredith/ Moment; Eduardo Fuster/Uig; Danita Delimont/Gallo Images/Getty Images Plus; **U8:** John S Lander/Lightrocket; Mike Hewitt/Getty Images Sport; Julian Finney/ Getty Images Sport; Harry How/Getty Images Sport; Pengpeng/E+; South China Morning Post; Soren Haldthe Image Bank/Getty Images Plus; Johner Images; Bananastock/Getty Images Plus; Cavan Images; Gradyreese/E+; Caiaimage; Stevica Mrdja/Eyeem; Severin Schweiger/Cultura; Nastasic/E+; Urbancow/E+; Solstock/E+; Paul Bradbury/Ojo Images; Flashpop/Digitalvision; John P Kelly/ The Image Bank/Getty Images Plus; Kaori Ando/Image Source; Stockbyte; Mike Harrington/Photodisc; Marina Herrmann/Moment; Highwaystarz-Photography/ iStock/Getty Images Plus; Viewstock; Zubin Shroff/Taxi/Getty Images Plus; **U9:** Alexander Manton; Andrewmedina/E+; Monkeybusinessimages/iStock/Getty Images Plus; Yellow Dog Productions/DigitalVision; Rostislavv/iStock Editorial/ Getty Images Plus; Baona/iStock/Getty Images Plus; Uppercut Images/Getty Images Plus; Lawrence Worcester/Lonely Planet Images/Getty Images Plus; Hola Images; Laflor/E+; Ajr_Images/iStock/Getty Images Plus; Fangxianuo/E+; VCG/Visual China Group; Paolo Vercesi/500Px; Hiya Images/Corbis/VCG; Hero Images; Jose Luis Pelaez Inc/Digitalvision; Jessica Holden Photography/Moment Open; The Lighthouse Film Co, Inc./Corbis/Getty Images Plus; Morsa Images/ Digitalvision; Shannon Fagan/The Image Bank/Getty Images Plus; **U10:** Brauns/ E+; Peopleimages/E+; Westend61; Stockbyte; Hero Images; Mstudioimages/ E+; Recep-Bg/E+; Seanshot/iStock/Getty Images Plus; Caiaimage; Jose Luis Pelaez Inc/Digitalvision; **U11:** Svetikd/E+; Vera Anderson/Wireimage; Pascal Le Segretain/Getty Images Entertainment; Franco Origlia/Getty Images Entertainment; Astrid Stawiarz/Getty Images Entertainment; Robert Frerck/The Image Bank/Getty Images Plus; Gilaxia/E+; PeopleImages/E+; Jack Vartoogian/ Archive Photos; Jon Feingersh Photography Inc/DigitalVision; Vgajic/E+; Hero Images; M-Imagephotography/iStock/Getty Images Plus; Barcroft Media; Jim Spellman/WireImage; Phillip Faraone/Getty Images Entertainment; Visual China Group; Rich Fury/Getty Images Entertainment; Adri/iStock/Getty Images Plus; Jessica Peterson; **U12:** Marabelo/iStock; David Clapp/The Image Bank/Getty Images Plus; John Elk/Lonely Planet Images/Getty Images Plus; Neil Holmes/ Photographer'S Choice/Getty Images Plus; Martin Harvey/Corbis Nx/Getty Images Plus; Cormon Francis/Hemis.Fr; Westend61; Mattis Quinn/Eyeem; Patricia Hamilton/Moment; Paul A. Souders/Corbis Documentary/Getty Images Plus; Ed Freeman/Stone/Getty Images Plus; Du Boisberranger Jean/Hemis.Fr; Rafal_Kubiak/iStock/Getty Images Plus; Antonio Luiz Hamdan/Photographer'S Choice/Getty Images Plus; Keith Levit/Design Pics; Marcus Lindstrom/E+; Artmarie/iStock/Getty Images Plus; Morsa Images/E+; Michael Blann/Stone/Getty Images Plus; Mysticenergy/E+; Matteo Colombo/Digitalvision; Wolfgang Kaehler/ Lightrocket; Manuel Sulzer/Cultura; Shannon Fagan/Photodisc; **C:** Jamie Grill; Aldomurillo/iStock/Getty Images Plus; **V:** John Kelly; Caiaimage; Tom Merton/ Ojo Images; Guvendemir/iStock/Getty Images Plus; Erik Isakson; Dougal Waters/ Digitalvision; Michael Blann/Digitalvision; Peter Muller/Cultura; John Moore/ Getty Images News; Yenwen/E+; Daniel Mcgarrah/Photolibrary/Getty Images Plus; Justin Sullivan/Getty Images News; Xixinxing; Darrin Klimek/Digitalvision; Adventtr/E+; Sally Williams Photography/Photolibrary/Getty Images Plus; ATU Images/Photographer'S Choice/Getty Images Plus; Westend61; Akepong Srichaichana/Eyeem; Rob White Photography/Photolibrary/Getty Images Plus; Thanatham Piriyakarnjanakul/Eyeem; Aerostato/iStock/Getty Images Plus; Bruno Crescia Photography Inc/First Light/Getty Images Plus; Ljupco/iStock/ Getty Images Plus; Zachary Sheldon/Design Pics/First Light/Getty Images Plus; Otmarw/iStock/Getty Images Plus; Design Pics; Thomas Barwick/Stone/Getty Images Plus; Slavica/iStock/Getty Images Plus; Maisie Paterson/The Image Bank/Getty Images Plus; Technotr/iStock; Davelongmedia/E+; Thomas Barwick/ Digitalvision; Kali9/E+; Studiocasper/iStock/Getty Images Plus; Fly-Jet/iStock/ Getty Images Plus; Zhaubasar/iStock/Getty Images Plus; Mawielobob/iStock/ Getty Images Plus; Ng Sok Lian/Eyeem; Mevans/E+; Digipub/Moment; Alle12/E+.

The following images are sourced from other Sourced/libraries.

Commissioned photography by Gareth Boden.

Illustrations by QBS Learning; Adrian Barclay; Mark Bird; Mark Duffin; John Goodwin; KJA Artists; Dusan Lakicevic; Jerome Mireault; Gavin Reece; Martin Sanders; David Semple; Sean Sims; Marie-Eve Tremblay; Gary Venn; Roger Penwill.

Typeset by QBS Learning.

Audio by John Marshall Media.

Corpus Development of this publication has made use of the Cambridge English Corpus(CEC). The CEC is a computer database of contemporary spoken and written English, which currently stands at over one billion words. It includes British English, American English and other varieties of English. It also includes the Cambridge Learner Corpus, developed in collaboration with the University of Cambridge ESOL Examinations. Cambridge University Press has built up the CEC to provide evidence about language use that helps us to produce better language teaching materials.

English Profile This product is informed by English Vocabulary Profile, built as part of English Profile, a collaborative program designed to enhance the learning, teaching and assessment of English worldwide. Its main funding partners are Cambridge University Press and Cambridge Assessment English and its aim is to create a "profile" for English, linked to the Common European Framework of Reference for Languages (CEFR). English Profile outcomes, such as the English Vocabulary Profile, will provide detailed information about the language that learners can be expected to demonstrate at each CEFR level, offering a clear benchmark for learners' proficiency. For more information, please visit www.englishprofile.org.

CALD The Cambridge Advanced Learner's Dictionary is the world's most widely used dictionary for learners of English. Including all the words and phrases that learners are likely to come across, it also has easy-to-understand definitions and example sentences to show how the word is used in context. The Cambridge Advanced Learner's Dictionary is available online at dictionary.cambridge.org.

Shaftesbury Road, Cambridge CB2 8EA, United Kingdom

One Liberty Plaza, 20th Floor, New York, NY 10006, USA

477 Williamstown Road, Port Melbourne, VIC 3207, Australia

314–321, 3rd Floor, Plot 3, Splendor Forum, Jasola District Centre, New Delhi – 110025, India

103 Penang Road, #05-06/07, Visioncrest Commercial, Singapore 238467

Cambridge University Press & Assessment is a department of the University of Cambridge.

We share the University's mission to contribute to society through the pursuit of education, learning and research at the highest international levels of excellence.

www.cambridge.org
Information on this title: www.cambridge.org/9781108862479

First published 2022

20 19 18 17 16 15 14 13 12 11 10 9 8 7 6 5

Printed in Poland by Opolgraf

A catalogue record for this publication is available from the British Library

ISBN 978-1-108-81751-6 Elementary Student's Book with eBook
ISBN 978-1-108-79716-0 Elementary Student's Book A with eBook
ISBN 978-1-108-79717-7 Elementary Student's Book B with eBook
ISBN 978-1-108-85046-9 Elementary Student's Book with Digital Pack
ISBN 978-1-108-86244-8 Elementary Student's Book A with Digital Pack
ISBN 978-1-108-86247-9 Elementary Student's Book B with Digital Pack
ISBN 978-1-108-81755-4 Elementary Workbook with Answers
ISBN 978-1-108-81756-1 Elementary Workbook A with Answers
ISBN 978-1-108-81757-8 Elementary Workbook B with Answers
ISBN 978-1-108-81758-5 Elementary Workbook without Answers
ISBN 978-1-108-81759-2 Elementary Workbook A without Answers
ISBN 978-1-108-81760-8 Elementary Workbook B without Answers
ISBN 978-1-108-81761-5 Elementary Full Contact with eBook
ISBN 978-1-108-81762-2 Elementary Full Contact A with eBook
ISBN 978-1-108-81763-9 Elementary Full Contact B with eBook
ISBN 978-1-108-85051-3 Elementary Full Contact with Digital Pack
ISBN 978-1-108-85054-4 Elementary Full Contact A with Digital Pack
ISBN 978-1-108-86243-1 Elementary Full Contact B with Digital Pack
ISBN 978-1-108-79719-1 Elementary Teacher's Book with Digital Pack
ISBN 978-1-108-79723-8 Elementary Presentation Plus

Additional resources for this publication at www.cambridge.org/americanempower